Feed *your* FAMILY

FAST, HEALTHY MEALS

$10 -ON-

A DAY

Feed *your* FAMILY

FAST, HEALTHY MEALS

$10 -ON- A DAY

LINDA WEST ECKHARDT

96 95 94 93   10 9 8 7 6 5 4 3 2 1

This book is revised from *All American Gumbo* by Linda West
Eckhardt, published in 1983 by Texas Monthly Press.

This is a Peregrine Smith Book, published by
Gibbs Smith, Publisher
P.O. Box 667
Layton, Utah 84041

Design by Randall Smith Associates
Printed in the U.S.A.

Library of Congress Cataloging-in-Publication Data

Eckhardt, Linda West, 1939-
Feed your family on $10 a day / Linda West Eckhardt.
p. cm.
Includes index.
ISBN 0-87905-582-0 (pbk.)
1. Low budget cookery. 2. Marketing (Home economics) I. Title.
II. Title: Feed your family on ten dollars a day.
TX652.E343 1993
641.5'52—dc20   93-2196
                                           CIP

▼

*Dedicated to the memory of my mother,
Bessie Lee Wood, who fed our family
on $10 a week when she had to.*

▲

Contents

Introduction

▼

I know it's possible to feed a family of four on $10 a day, because I've done it off and on now for ten years. Our budget goes from tight to tighter, depending on those unexpected expenses that do seem to jump up when it's least convenient. And when push comes to shove, I can always fall back on a system that works for saving grocery money while our family still eats well.

One Thanksgiving, for example, our dumb dog turned over the neighbor's garbage and had his own dinner of leftover salmon. Two weeks and $550 later, he was back home from the vet's. We learned the hard way that salmon is poison to dogs. Merry Christmas. We had to cinch in our money belts in every department just to pay that bill.

For that once-a-year special Christmas dinner, I had no choice but to hunt for a bargain turkey, cook root vegetables, and bake a pie from the green-tomato mincemeat I'd canned last summer from the garden. The whole dinner cost about $12. And you want to know something? We all agreed it was the best Christmas dinner we'd had in years. And we had leftovers for days after.

I want to share with you the shopping strategy I came up with several years ago that works for me when I must cut back on the grocery bill.

I divide the weekly menu into seven categories and only go to the grocery store once a week, taking a list of nothing more than the weekly staples we need. While there, I check specials, buying the main item from the seven categories to take advantage of in-store specials and seasonal buys. Once home, I figure out what to do with my bargains. This way we never get bored eating the same old thing, I don't have to spend time I haven't got devising menus and shopping lists, and shopping and cooking become an adventure and a glorious pleasure.

This means that once a week our dinner entrée will be:

1. Fish or Shellfish
2. Pasta or Rice
3. Poultry
4. Vegetarian
5. Red Meats
6. Beans or Peas
7. Eggs or Cheese

But what about breakfast and lunch you ask? Can I still make it on $10 a day serving three meals? By making some simple decisions, the answer is an unqualified yes.

First of all, skip all those oversugared, oversalted, overpriced breakfast cereals. Choose a cereal your family will eat—say oatmeal or Malt-O-Meal, and cook that most weekdays for breakfast. Too much trouble you say? Try it in the microwave. Even a third grader can do it.

As for lunch, leftovers from the recipes in this book frequently make delicious brown bag lunches for adults. Otherwise, apply the K.I.S.S. principle: keep it simple stupid—a sandwich, a piece of fruit, a carton of yogurt. You'll save money, calories, and your health, both for you and your children.

Save restaurant visits for special occasions. The reason high-priced restaurant food tastes so good is that they use beaucoup fat in everything. Save money. Save fat. Save your arteries. Cook from scratch at home for most meals.

And by the way, I don't think of this $10-a-day regimen as something I'm going to have to do the rest of my life. Think of it as putting your grocery budget on a diet. Get the household budget back in trim, and you can begin to enjoy eating out again.

Necessity being the mother of invention, I can tell you that I devised this system only when I had to. I try to stay ahead of the curve because I am a food writer. And ten years ago, when everybody else was jumping on the extravagant '80s bandwagon, I looked down the road and went broke first. Actually, it was my husband's illness and early retirement that forced our family into a new way of life. With a husband and two sons still at home to feed, plus a daughter in college and a busy career of my own, the shift of responsibility to my shoulders seemed at times almost overwhelming.

Very quickly I learned that although I couldn't change the cost of the mortgage or the car payment, I could get control of the grocery budget. We also learned that even if we couldn't afford lots of movie tickets or trips to the beach, we could take inordinate pleasure at the table. Food became our central delight. And with that, came a strengthening of our family bond as we again sat around the dinner table together.

We learned firsthand what they mean when they say that peasants and kings have one thing in common: they both eat well.

Saving money at the table simply boils down to saving money at the grocery store and cooking without waste. We've all seen the knee-jerk directions that tell you to make out weekly menus, prepare a list and stick to it, leave the kids at home when you shop, use coupons, and shop several stores to get the best specials.

For me, this style of shopping presented a huge dilemma, because it was always kind of a draw which was in shorter supply—time or money. Besides: (A) I certainly don't have time to make menus for a week and probably wouldn't stick to them anyway. (B) I find lists as restricting as a straight jacket.

Working moms get little enough time with their kids; therefore, I decided to engage my boys in the process of shopping and cooking supper to give us time together. With a little strategy, it helped me get the shopping and cooking done and taught them good kitchen skills in the process. It also kept them away from television at least one afternoon.

When I devised this shopping strategy, I thought it was only for the tough times. But, I find it has changed forever the way I approach grocery shopping. It is possible to walk into a store with nothing more than the barest clue of what to eat for the coming week. Then quickly, easily, and with the greatest thrift, I can purchase the basis for a week's worth of meals that are the healthiest possible.

I work the perimeter of the store first, where the fresh foods are.

I buy the most interesting-looking red meat I see on sale: say a pot roast or lamb chops. I see what's doing on ice in the fish counter. Usually, that's what we eat that night. Fish cooking's quick, it's healthy and this way I don't have fish lurking in the back of the refrigerator leaping into rot before I know it.

The rest of the week's menu falls into place: a dried bean dinner one night, chicken the next, a pasta dish another. Once around for an egg or cheese meal, and a vegetarian meal made from what looks best in the produce section rounds out the week.

The basic philosophy behind this strategy says that I want to feed my family a broad and varied diet of healthy foods that will not only be good for them, but taste good while being economical. After having written about food for twenty years, I know that food fads come and go, and that your best bet for sound nutrition is to aim for a diet of primarily unprocessed foods from all the basic food groups—in moderation.

The good news is that this also happens to be the cheapest way to eat. Stay away from overprocessed foods and you will save not only money but your health.

The U.S. Department of Agriculture considers $89 a week a thrifty weekly food budget for a family of four with two preschoolers. Following my plan, you can lop nearly twenty bucks off of that figure with no appreciable loss in interesting, nutritional meals, even if your kids are playing on the high-school football team.

Think about it: what's the most expensive item in the grocery store—not counting the luxury-priced processed foods? It's red meat. How often does your family eat red meat? Serving it only once a week will save money, yet still provide your family with the necessary

iron and micro-nutrients most efficiently conveyed by red meats. Eat a lean red meat entrée weekly and you'll also notice fewer cravings for high-fat, expensive meat meals.

Another part of my strategy is to make one-dish meals during the week to save time and money. Many of the recipes in this book are a meal-in-one. In other words, I find that if I use meat, fish, eggs, or cheese as flavorings in dishes that stand on a basis of pasta, rice, or vegetables, I've served fewer ounces of high-priced foods and improved our nutrition in the process by making complex carbohydrates the real basis for the meal.

Think about the peasant cultures of the world, how they eat: Chinese, Italian, Mexican—to name just a few of America's favorite ethnic cuisines. These food styles devised by wily peasant cooks relied on grain or vegetable bases tuned up by bites of meat, poultry, or fish. It's a healthy way to cook and live, plus, it's cheap. And the bonus is that if dinner is cooked in one pot, you don't end up with a sink full of dirty dishes. It's a win-win solution.

But back to the grocery store. Here are some tips I've learned:

▶ Use coupons only for foods you would ordinarily buy anyway. Most manufacturers' coupons are designed to introduce you to new processed foods that are overpriced, overchemicaled, and undervalued in the nutrition.

▶ Don't try to buy everything every week. If you know a good warehouse store a bit further from home that has bargain prices, swing through it about once a month to pick up the bulk sale necessities: pasta, beans, cleaning supplies, and paper products.

- ▶ If your family is small, team up with a neighbor to split a jumbo package of rice, toilet paper, or canned tomatoes. You can save as much as 66% of the cost buying in bulk.

- ▶ Don't rely only on the neighborhood supermarket for best buys. Farmer's markets frequently offer in-season local produce that is fresher, cheaper, and more flavorful than that trucked in by a supermarket chain. Again, team up with a neighbor and split a bushel of peaches or a peck of pears. You'll enjoy your meals more if you begin to eat seasonally, and you'll note that wonderful law of supply and demand: when produce is the most plentiful, it's also the cheapest. This is when you can begin to enjoy table debauchery—a dinner of nothing more than a mountain of just-picked asparagus with a loaf of crusty French bread. Later, in high summer, make a dinner of waffles with fresh-picked blackberries. Heaps and heaps of blackberries.

- ▶ Don't throw food away. Use leftovers in ways that make them new again. Many of the recipes in this book actually taste better the second day. In these instances, our family is more than happy to eat a dish two days in a row.

- ▶ At the grocery store, skip the junk food: no chips, soft drinks, candy, cookies, rice casseroles, sugared cereals, or frozen dinners. Make your own. You can, for example, make tortilla chips by simply cutting a 35¢ pack of corn tortillas into wedges, then seasoning them with salt or flavorings, and toasting them in the oven on a cookie sheet coated with cooking spray. For 35¢ you get at least two bucks worth of chips. You don't get a bunch of chemical preservatives either.

- ▶ Pay cash for your groceries. There's nothing like the reality check of counting out dollar bills to pay for something. Keep your checkbook at home and don't even think about grabbing the plastic.

Along these lines, get to know what items cost. If something you normally buy is too expensive this week, skip it. Practice Eckhardt's golden rule: When in doubt, substitute or leave it out. Plug a substitution into your recipe and you may even improve it. (See appendix for an exhaustive list of substitutes.)

And finally, you'll see that lavish amounts of stinginess can be fun. You can get the same pleasure at making sumptuous meals spending less money as you do from buying great clothes from the outlet malls. It's like a game actually. You can beat the system, eat well, and have fun doing it.

Stick with me and I'll teach you how to make great cut-to-the-bone-appetit.

Linda West Eckhardt
January 1993

Fish and Shellfish

▼

*T*he widespread availability of fresh fish in this country is a moderately new addition to grocery stores, unless you live on the coast. Because of that, this dinner entrée is one that many people pass over. However, fish is one of the real bargains in good taste—almost pure protein, little fat or cholesterol, and usually priced within the range of the most stringent budget. It's even good out of a can.

The variety available in seafood is staggering, although selection and price depend greatly on where you live. When I lived in Houston, we made a regular pilgrimage to Kemah, where we would walk out on the hot steamy docks to buy shrimp right off the boat, usually from 50¢ to $1.00 a pound. Now that I live on the Pacific Coast, the offerings from the sea are different. This year the salmon run was bounteous and even Safeway sold whole fish for less than $1.00 a pound. Regardless of what fishes are available to you, the principles for cooking fish remain the same, and using these recipes, you can substitute whatever fish you prefer.

Since fish is the most fragile of meats, the first task is to choose a fresh one, and this usually means choosing a reliable fishmonger. To assess the fish: when buying a whole fish, look it in the eye. If the fish isn't laid out on ice, staring back at you with a clear, unblinking eye, pass on. If the eye is sunken or cloudy, the fish is beginning to deteriorate. When buying fillets, the quickest test for freshness is a good deep breath. If you get the least hint of ammonia in that whiff, put it back. Grocers are going to hate me for saying this, but if I had no

choice but prepackaged fish in the refrigerated counter, I would punch a hole in the cellophane and smell the fish carefully. If there is little or no odor, I'll take it.

When you look at the table of contents for this chapter, you will note that certain fishes are conspicuous by their absence. You will find no lobster, no crab, no scallops, and no shrimp. The reason is price. Unless you live where these shellfish are caught, they cost too much for this budget collection.

One fish you ought to enjoy while it's still inexpensive, is squid. Packaged primarily in Monterey, California, and distributed frozen all over the country, squid is one of the most delicate and interesting fishes. Indeed, there is a movement afoot to make squid a gourmet delicacy. Squid is now reasonably priced (around $1.00 a pound), but the packers hope to raise this price and give squid a luxury-food status. I am beginning to see cleaned squid "steaks" for $5.00 a pound. Because squid is easy to clean, buying it whole (fresh or frozen) and cleaning it myself is more economical.

The oyster recipes in this section assume that you are going to make one of those parsimonious jars feed four people. Fortunately, oysters are so rich and flavorful that they do not suffer when nestled in a bed of other ingredients.

Good old canned tuna is used in **Tuna Update** in the Pasta and Rice chapter. Do try this new look at an old favorite. Tuna is good and it is cheap.

Fish fillets, flash frozen in a solid one-pound block, are the only fish—other than squid—that I ever consider from the frozen food section. Used within two or three weeks and cooked in a flavorful liquid of some kind, frozen fish provides a good meal.

There is one thing to keep in mind when cooking fish, whether you're cooking it on stovetop or in the oven: too much heat for too long a time can turn even the best fish into styrofoam. Keep the heat low. Cook the fish just until it loses that translucent look. Stick a fork into the fish; the moment the meat is opaque and flaky, take it off the heat and serve—on hot plates, please. Cooking fresh fish requires your undivided attention. Keep an eye on the fish, an eye on the heat, and an eye on the clock, and you will turn out a splendid meal that will have them begging for more.

Hangtown Fry

▼

FEEDS 4 IN 15 MINUTES
About 75¢ per serving

In the California gold rush, inflation got completely out of hand. Eggs were sometimes sold for a dollar apiece. Oysters, which many flatlanders had only heard about, were equally high-priced. So if a fellow was feeling flush from a good find and wanted a night out on the town, he might order the priciest thing on the menu—Hangtown Fry— and pay for it with gold dust. Now that a jar or can of oysters costs less than $2.00, and eggs being as cheap as they are, this gold-rush dish is a bargain.

Californians are quick to lay claim to this splendid frontier gourmet dish, but I have a sneaking suspicion that the basis for it may have moved west just as surely as the gold seekers did. Just think for a moment of the name of this dish. The word fries was a cowboy's vernacular for testicles, otherwise known as "mountain oysters." If I were making up this story here's what I would say.

There was an old cowboy cook who was sick of puttin' up with the complaints of cowboys. One night, while sittin' around the campfire, the outfit was host to a guest—a feller moving west, going to seek his fortune in golden California. While the cook was a-sittin' there listenin' to the stranger's stories and rubbing his arthritic joints, one of the young whippersnappers made some nasty crack about his sinkers, claimin' his biscuits could kill a mockingbird at 50 yards. The cook was just plum fed up; so the next morning before breakfast, he saddled up with the gold seeker and left those hungry cowboys to fend for themselves.

After many adventures crossing the desert and the Sierra, these two fellers got to California, where the cook opened a little cafe in a tent right at the foot of the mountains, in a makeshift town that had a reputation for quick, sure western-style justice. The town was aptly named Hangtown. Our cook was sweatin' plenty, hopin' to avoid a dose of this justice. At least when he was cookin' for cowboys, they had to eat what he put before them. Here in the Wild West, tempers were short and nooses were long.

The thing of it was, he had plenty of hungry customers with gold dust in their pockets, but he was short on supplies as well as ideas until this old Portuguese came up from San Francisco. He was offerin' to sell our restaurateur some ursters; our nervous businessman bought. Course they weren't as good as the mountain oysters our cook was used to, but he applied his old cowboy recipe to these newfangled things, priced them way up to bluff the yahoos, and much to his surprise, found them the most popular thing on the menu. Why, the fellers were soon attributing wondrous powers to this dish. They had hardly finished a plateful before they were chasing around the faded doves who had drifted West with the strike. They were soon claimin' it gave them strength to work the streams from daylight to dark. Our old cook took this in stride, and when confronted with his happy customers, just snorted and said, "Any fool would have knowed that."

4 slices bacon
7 eggs
12 ounces oysters, drained
Salt and pepper to taste
2 tablespoons butter or margarine
Cracker meal, bread crumbs, or a mixture of
    cornmeal and flour
½ cup milk

Fry bacon until crisp; drain. Beat one egg. Salt and pepper drained oysters. Dip each one into the meal, into the beaten egg, and into the meal again. Heat butter in a 10-inch skillet over medium-low heat, frying oysters gently until golden brown on one side. While they are frying, beat the remaining 6 eggs with milk, salt, and pepper. Count the oysters and divide crisp bacon into as many pieces as there are oysters. Turn oysters; top each with a piece of crisp bacon. Pour in egg mixture and cook gently until set. Do not stir, but occasionally lift the edges of the mixture with a spatula, tipping the skillet to let the uncooked egg run under. Once the eggs are set, set the skillet under the broiler to brown the top; watch carefully so they don't overbrown. Serve on a hot platter. Good with french fries.

Oyster Loaf
▼
FEEDS 4 IN 15 MINUTES
About 75¢ per serving

How can you make one jar of oysters feed four people when, if the truth were told, you could eat them all yourself, raw, right out of the jar? You can do what the New Orleanians have been doing for years: you can make an oyster loaf using the simple recipe below.

1 1-pound loaf day-old unsliced French bread
Butter or margarine, softened
16 ounces oysters, drained
½ cup Cornmeal
Salt and pepper to taste
2 tablespoons cooking oil
Dill pickles, sliced

Red Sauce:
¼ cup catsup
¼ cup mayonnaise
¼ teaspoon prepared mustard
1 tablespoon horseradish
Juice of half a lemon
1 teaspoon Worcestershire sauce
4 drops Tabasco sauce

Preheat oven to 300° F. Slice bread horizontally and lay the two halves faceup on a cookie sheet. Hollow each half and tear the removed bread into small pieces; set aside. Lightly coat the cavity with margarine, then replace the torn pieces. Toast the opened loaf in the oven while making the red sauce and frying the oysters.

Heat oil in a 10-inch skillet over medium heat while you salt and pepper the oysters then dredge them in cornmeal. Fry oysters until they are golden on both sides (no longer than 3 minutes). Drain on paper towels.

To make red sauce, combine remaining ingredients in a small bowl. Set aside. Take bread from oven and remove loose bread pieces. Place fried oysters in the cavity of one half. Top with dill pickles. Cover with red sauce. Mound the toasted bread pieces over all, then place remaining bread half on top and place in the oven to warm thoroughly (5–10 minutes). Slice loaf and serve hot.

Lovely Latin Fillets

▼

FEEDS 4 IN 2 HOURS AND 30 MINUTES
(INCLUDING MARINATING TIME)
About 75¢ per serving

Frozen fish fillets, sold in a one-pound solid block, are a good affordable buy at the grocery store. Perch or cod are less expensive than sole. You can thaw them in several ways. The orderly, civilized way is to take them out of the freezer and place them, still in the package, in the refrigerator section about 24 hours before you're ready to use them. Who are we kidding? If you decide on fish 40 minutes before dinner is served, either thaw them in the microwave or run lukewarm water over them until they separate easily.

1 pound frozen perch or cod fillets, thawed
Salt to taste
2 cloves garlic, pressed
Juice of a lemon
2 tablespoons olive oil
1 medium onion, sliced thin
1 28-oz. can whole tomatoes, drained and chopped
1 fresh jalapeño, seeded and chopped fine
⅛ teaspoon dried oregano
⅛ teaspoon dried thyme
2 bay leaves
¼ teaspoon sugar
2 tablespoons margarine
Cilantro or parsley for garnish

Place fillets or other one layer deep in a 9x9-inch glass baking dish. Sprinkle with salt and press garlic over, gently rubbing salt and garlic into fillets. Add lemon juice. Cover and marinate at room temperature for 1 hour, turning the fish several times.

About 30 minutes before serving time, heat the olive oil in a heavy 10-inch skillet over medium heat and gently sauté the onion until translucent. Add tomatoes, jalapeño, oregano, thyme, bay leaves, and sugar. Simmer uncovered for 10 minutes, stirring occasionally. Pour this sauce into a bowl and reserve on the back of the stove.

Add margarine to the same skillet over high heat. When the margarine sizzles, remove fillets from marinade and sauté over high heat until golden on both sides, turning only once. Discard marinade.

Remove fillets to warmed serving plate, pour sauce over, and sprinkle with chopped cilantro or parsley. Serve with fluffy rice.

Danielle's Tuna Apple Salad

▼

**FEEDS 4 IN 1 HOUR AND 10 MINUTES
(INCLUDES REFRIGERATION TIME)**
About 75¢ per serving

In the winter this looks and tastes great served on a bed of leafy kale.

1 12½-ounce can tuna chunks, packed in water
2 tart unpeeled apples, cored and chopped coarse
2 ribs celery, sliced diagonally
1 green onion and top, sliced
Salad greens

Combine tuna with apples, celery, and onion. Make dressing by mixing all remaining ingredients. Pour over tuna mixture. Cover and refrigerate at least 1 hour. Serve on a bed of salad greens.

Mexican Snapper

▼

FEEDS 4 IN 30 MINUTES
About $1.00 per serving

1 pound fresh or frozen red snapper fillets
Vegetable oil
½ teaspoon salt
¼ cup fresh cilantro or parsley leaves, crushed
½ teaspoon dried red pepper flakes
½ teaspoon dried oregano

1 green onion, chopped
1 sprig parsley, cut fine with scissors
Juice of 1 lime
1 avocado, peeled and cut into julienne strips

Preheat oven to 350° F. Oil a shallow baking dish large enough to hold the fillets without overlapping, then line bottom with fillets one layer deep, turning once to coat each side with oil. Salt to taste. Sprinkle with half the cilantro, pepper, oregano, onion, and parsley. Bake uncovered until the fish is flaky—about 20 minutes. Lift cooked fish to a warmed serving platter, pour lime juice over, arrange avocado slices on top, sprinkle with remaining onion mixture and serve.

MUSTARD BATTER FISH
Spread fish fillets (thawed or fresh) with plain prepared yellow mustard. Dredge in flour. Cook in a frying pan in hot oil until brown (about 4 minutes per side). Turn only once. Unbelievably simple and delicious.

Curried Fish Fillets

▼

FEEDS 4 IN 15 MINUTES
About 55¢ per serving

1 pound frozen fish fillets, thawed
¼ cup flour
1 tablespoon Madras curry powder
¼ pound margarine
⅓ cup sesame seeds or almonds (optional)

Separate fillets. Combine flour and curry. Dredge fillets in the mixture. Melt margarine in a 10-inch skillet over medium heat. Cook fillets, placing serving side down first and turning only once (about 4 minutes to the side). Fry until golden brown on both sides. Remove to heated platter. Add sesame seeds to remaining pan juices, stir to brown, then pour over the fish. Good with plain rice, a dish of sliced bananas, and maybe some sliced ripe tomatoes.

Louisiana Fish Fillets

▼

FEEDS 4 IN 1 HOUR AND 15 MINUTES
(INCLUDES MARINATING TIME)
About 70¢ per serving

1 pound frozen fish fillets, thawed
Juice of a lemon
¼ cup salad oil
½ cup flour
Salt and pepper to taste
½ cup milk
½ cup cornmeal
½ cup fresh parsley, chopped

Pour lemon juice over fillets and marinate in the refrigerator for at least 1 hour. About 15 minutes before serving time, heat oil in a 10-inch skillet over medium heat. Meanwhile, generously season flour with salt and pepper. Now dip fillets in milk, then in flour, then back in milk, and finally in cornmeal. Place in skillet, serving side down, and fry until golden brown (about 10 minutes), turning only once. Remove to warm serving plate. Place chopped parsley over fish and serve.

Tomato Fish Fillets

▼

FEEDS 4 IN 35 MINUTES
About 75¢ per serving

1 pound frozen fish fillets, thawed
1 tablespoon salad oil
1 onion, minced
½ cup cheddar cheese, grated
Salt and pepper to taste
1 6-ounce can tomato paste

Preheat oven to 350° F. Oil a shallow baking dish large enough to hold fillets without overlapping, and line the bottom with fillets, one layer deep. Combine onion, cheese, salt and pepper, and tomato paste. Spread over fish. Bake uncovered until fish flakes—about 20 minutes.

Box Shrimp Supper

▼

FEEDS 4 IN 15 MINUTES
About 59¢ per serving

This makes a dinner that won't heat up the kitchen or the cook and will keep the kids fed and happy. For savings at the supermarket, watch for the store brand of macaroni and cheese dinners to go on special. And compare the cost of canned shrimp to fresh; sometimes you can buy fresh a little cheaper, and the quality is far superior to canned.

2 teaspoons margarine
1 medium apple, cored, peeled, and diced
½ cup celery, sliced thin
1 teaspoon curry powder
1 7½-ounce box macaroni and cheese
½ cup 1% milk
4–4½ ounces cooked bay shrimp (canned or fresh)

In a medium skillet, heat margarine over medium-high heat, being careful not to burn. Sauté apple and celery with curry powder until they are brown. Set aside.

Meanwhile, in a medium saucepot, bring 2 quarts water to a boil and cook the macaroni until tender, about 6 minutes. (Note: the fat was used to sauté the apple instead of mixing it in the macaroni as box directions indicate.) Drain the macaroni, then mix with cheese packet, milk, sautéed apple and celery. Cook until creamy, then stir in the shrimp and heat through. Serve at once.

Pasta and Rice

▼

*I*n this chapter, you'll find a cross section of cuisine that spans several cultures and treatments of grain-based entrées, beginning with a light souffle version of macaroni and cheese and continuing through a wide variety of pasta and rice combinations. Remember that by combining grain with beans or cheese, you have a complete protein and can, if you wish, forego meat entirely for that meal. You will also note that there are good reasons for all those spaghetti dinners as fund-raisers. Pasta and rice main dishes can be dirt cheap and still satisfying.

The variety and choice in the pasta and rice department make this category a joy to explore. Once I saw dried red and green vegetable pasta bow ties and I scooped up a sack full to save for a quick Christmas Eve supper of Fettuccine Crema. It was good and cheap, quick, and festive to boot.

Cheesy Macaroni Soufflé

▼

FEEDS 4 IN 1 HOUR
About 80¢ per serving

1 cup uncooked macaroni
2 tablespoons margarine
3 tablespoons flour
½ teaspoon salt
½ teaspoon paprika
Dash of cayenne or red pepper
1¼ cups milk
1½ cups natural sharp cheddar cheese, shredded
3 eggs, separated

Preheat oven to 350° F. Grease a 2-quart casserole. Cook macaroni according to package directions; drain. Meanwhile, melt margarine in a large saucepan. Stir in flour, salt, paprika, and cayenne. Add milk to make a light roux. Cook and stir over moderate heat until thick. Remove from heat. Add cheese and stir to melt. Beat egg yolks until light. Slowly add to cheese sauce. Add drained macaroni. Beat egg whites until stiff. Fold into macaroni and cheese mixture. Pour into casserole. Bake 35–40 minutes or until center is firm to the touch when pressed lightly. Serve immediately.

Mexican Macaroni

▼

FEEDS 4 IN 40 MINUTES
About 60¢ per serving

1 cup uncooked macaroni
1 large onion, peeled and minced
1 green pepper (either mild chili or bell), seeded and chopped
2 tablespoons olive oil
1 16-ounce can stewed tomatoes
Salt and pepper
1 cup cheese, grated (cheddar, jack, or a mixture)
Cilantro or parsley, cut fine with scissors

Preheat oven to 350° F. Cook macaroni in boiling water according to package directions, but just until al dente; drain. Meanwhile, in a medium skillet over medium-high heat, sauté onion and pepper in olive oil until beginning to brown, then add tomatoes with juice. Reduce heat; cook and stir until sauce thickens, about 10 minutes. Salt and pepper to taste.

Place a layer of macaroni in a buttered casserole dish. Then add a layer of sauce, a sprinkle of cilantro or parsley, then grated cheese. Repeat layers. Bake 20 minutes or until bubbly and cheese is beginning to melt and brown.

Fettuccine Crema

▼

FEEDS 4 IN 30 MINUTES
About 65¢ per serving

When my son has his grade school buddies over for supper, I double this recipe. It's easy to the point of being embarrassing. You can have them in and out of the kitchen before all the mud has flaked off the bottom of their shoes, and they will invariably say, "Your mom sure can cook."

Last night, however, I almost ruined my reputation with the K-6 crowd. I served the plates in the kitchen, with pickled beets beside the noodles. Adults like pickled beets. The neighbor kid's digestion was ruined, however, in his effort to keep the pristine noodles away from that creeping pool of deadly red juice.

8 ounces egg noodles, uncooked
¼ pound margarine
1 cup evaporated milk (5.33-ounce can)
1 3-ounce package cream cheese
⅓ cup Parmesan cheese, grated

Cook noodles according to package directions; drain. Meanwhile, in a medium saucepan over the lowest heat, combine remaining ingredients. Stir to mix into a smooth sauce. Do not boil. Mix noodles with sauce and serve. Pass additional Parmesan at the table if you wish.

Mushrooms in the Straw & Hay

▼

FEEDS 6 IN 30 MINUTES
About 70¢ per serving

Looks good, tastes great. Good enough for company. For a special presentation, begin in the living room with Carpaccio and hot French bread. Move to the table, serve the pasta with a side dish of fresh tomato slices sprinkled with fresh sweet basil and vinaigrette. For dessert, a fresh peach drizzled with Marsala wine and served with strong black coffee.

2 tablespoons margarine
6 cloves garlic, crushed with the flat side of a knifeblade
1 pound mushrooms, sliced thin
8 ounces thin spinach noodles, uncooked
8 ounces thin egg noodles, uncooked
1 cup evaporated milk (5.33-ounce can)
¼ cup chicken broth
½ cup Romano or Parmesan cheese, grated (or a combination)

Fill two large saucepans with 4 quarts of water and bring to a boil. Meanwhile, in a 10-inch skillet heat margarine over medium-high heat and sauté garlic until it begins to brown. Add mushrooms and sauté until lightly browned. Set aside.

Cook green and white noodles separately in boiling water according to package directions, eliminating salt; drain. Don't overcook! Combine in a warm bowl.

Meanwhile, add the milk and broth to

mushrooms and bring to a boil. Remove from the heat. Stir in cheese. Pour over noodles and toss to mix. Pass additional cheese at the table if you wish.

Tuna Update!

▼

FEEDS 4 IN 25 MINUTES
About $1.00 per serving

You remember it: tuna noodle casserole (the color and texture of wet clay). Mothers served it on Friday nights. It was the standby of Girl Scout camp. It was the second thing you were taught in junior-high home economics: one can of tuna fish, one can of mushroom soup, a package of egg noodles. The fancier versions might have had bits of onion or bell pepper; and for special occasions, the top might be sprinkled with cheddar cheese or crumbled, possibly stale, potato chips. (Enough salt to make your vessels slam shut.) Here's an updated version—what an improvement!

12 ounces thin noodles, linguine, or spaghetti, uncooked
1 lemon
⅛ pound margarine
2 tablespoons olive oil
2 large bell peppers (one red and one green) cut in julienne strips
4 cloves garlic, pressed or chopped fine
¼ teaspoon dried red pepper, crushed
¾ cup chicken broth
16 ½-ounce can tuna chunks, drained
¾ cup parsley, chopped fine

In a medium-large saucepan, bring 5 quarts of lightly salted water to a boil. Add noodles and cook according to package directions; drain, rinse briefly with cold water and let stand in a colander.

Meanwhile, using a zester or a potato peeler, thinly pare peel from the lemon. Cut peel into fine slivers. Juice lemon and set juice aside.

Heat margarine and olive oil in a 10-inch skillet over medium-high heat. Add bell pepper strips, garlic, and crushed red pepper; cook, stirring 1 minute. Lift out bell peppers with a slotted spoon and set aside.

Add lemon juice and chicken broth to the margarine. Bring to a boil. Add tuna to boiling liquid and heat thoroughly. Try not to break up the chunks. When tuna is heated through, remove from liquid and place with the bell peppers.

Add noodles to boiling pan juices. Heat, turning with two forks, until pasta is hot. Pour pasta and sauce into a serving bowl, top with lemon slivers, bell peppers, tuna, and parsley. Toss to serve.

FROZEN CHICKEN BROTH

This is one more recipe that makes good use of chicken broth, which you should have frozen from the last time you poached a chicken. I just pour this broth into a plastic container, freeze, then thaw what I need in the microwave. If you don't use a microwave, you can freeze the broth in a metal container, set it in boiling water and thaw what you need, then replace the frozen block in the freezer for another day.

Basic Marinara Sauce

▼

FEEDS 4 IN 20 MINUTES
About 35¢ per serving

I won't bore you with some long treatise on tomato sauce, but as recently as 150 years ago, the tomato was considered mildly to moderately poisonous. The habit of cooking tomato sauce all day may have evolved from the belief that any cooking effort short of a whole day might make it the Last Supper.

Today we know better. I can make a perfectly lovely marinara sauce in 20 minutes. You can, too. It tastes good, it's easy, and it's cheap. Those Italian housewives know this. Who knows? Maybe they just told the old man they'd been cooking it all day.

¼ cup olive oil
2 small onions, peeled and chopped fine
2 cloves garlic, pressed
1 28-ounce can tomatoes
1 teaspoon dried sweet basil
½ teaspoon sugar
Salt and pepper to taste
1 pound pasta

Heat oil in a 10-inch skillet; add onions and garlic, cooking until translucent. Chop tomatoes into the pan and add the juice. Season to taste with basil, sugar, and salt and pepper. Cook, stirring over medium heat for about 20 minutes. If the sauce is too thin after this time, raise the heat and cook until it reaches a catsuplike consistency. If you want a perfectly smooth sauce, puree in processor. Meanwhile, cook pasta according to package directions, and get out the Parmesan. Tear some salad greens for a salad. Hunt up a little red wine. Got a checkered tablecloth? No, this is going too far. But you get the idea.

You can vary the sauce by adding a half pound of hamburger, browned in a separate skillet. Or you can make some meatballs by mixing bread crumbs and egg and a touch of nutmeg with the meat. I've also tossed squid into the sauce for the last two minutes of the cooking time. It was delicious. Of course, squid exudes a lot of water, so you must have the sauce quite reduced if you plan to add squid. See how endless the possibilities are? A little turkey? A little tuna? What do you have?

For the marinara sauce, pop two frozen olive oil and basil cubes into the skillet and begin from there. As the cube melts, the basil looks as brilliant and green as if it were fresh picked. Basil, sorrel, and cilantro all freeze well in oil.

FREEZING FRESH HERBS

For other interesting versions of basic marinara sauce, experiment with fresh herbs. Fresh parsley, for example, costs about 20¢ a bunch in most grocery stores. Stick it in a jar with water so that it sits like a posey on the refrigerator shelf, cover the leaves with plastic wrap, and just pinch off what you need. To keep fresh herbs over a long period, try freezing them. Pack each cell of an ice cube tray with the herb—chopped fine—and add enough olive oil or water to fill the tray. Cover with plastic and freeze. Once frozen, you can pop out the ice cubes and store them in a plastic bag. Now you have perfectly preserved herbs—about a tablespoon at a time.

Spaghetti and Spice

▼

FEEDS 4 IN 20 MINUTES
About 65¢ per serving

12 ounces spaghetti
¼ cup olive oil
8 cloves garlic, peeled and divided
1 cup parsley, finely cut with scissors
1 cup chicken broth
Fresh-ground black pepper
Parmesan cheese, grated

Cook spaghetti according to package directions until al dente (just barely tender). An easy way to determine this stage is to pull out a strand after 6 or 7 minutes, cut it, and look closely at the cut edge. If the strand has a hard white core, you need to cook the spaghetti a moment more. But if the strand has a creamy sameness all across its diameter, immediately stop the cooking—otherwise the edges will begin to dissolve into the water and you've got a pot of glue. Drain well.

Meanwhile, in a 6-inch skillet, heat oil on medium-high heat. Thin-slice half the garlic cloves and fry in olive oil until brown, then set aside. Press the other half of the garlic cloves onto the parsley; set aside.

Put the drained spaghetti back in the pot, mix with oil and garlic, and add chicken broth. Simmer about 5 minutes. Stir in parsley and garlic and serve in soup bowls with plenty of black pepper and Parmesan on top.

Noodles with Szechuan Sauce

▼

FEEDS 2 IN 30 MINUTES
About 55¢ per serving

Learn to make homemade noodles and you can vary this recipe a million ways. Serve them with olive oil and garlic, in chicken noodle soup, under spaghetti sauce. Eat them plain with butter. To tell the truth, homemade noodles are heaven.

Noodles:
½ cup unbleached flour
1 egg
Pinch salt

Soup:
2 cups chicken broth
2 green onions, finely chopped

Szechuan Peanut Sauce:
2 tablespoons chunky peanut butter
1 teaspoon chili powder
4 cloves garlic, minced
½ teaspoon hot chili flakes
1 tablespoon vegetable oil
2 tablespoons soy sauce, reduced sodium
1 teaspoon sesame oil
1 tablespoon fresh ginger, chopped
½ teaspoon white or rice vinegar
½ teaspoon salt
1 teaspoon sugar
(continued)

To make the noodles, combine flour and egg in the food processor with salt. Process about 30 seconds using the steel blade, until the dough forms a ball that rides the blade around. Then let the dough rest in the bowl.

Meanwhile, wipe counter top, then coat lightly with flour. Roll the dough out into a very thin circle, about 14-inches across. Keep turning and rotating the dough so that it will be easy to handle. Leave it to dry a few minutes then cut into thin noodles using a knife or noodle cutter. Hang the noodles over a chair back or rod to dry a few minutes while you make the sauce and begin to boil the soup.

In a medium soup pan, combine chicken broth with half the green onions and bring to a boil.

Meanwhile, mix remaining ingredients to make the sauce. Set this aside.

Drop the noodles into boiling broth and cook 2–3 minutes or just until tender. Divide the noodles and broth into two soup bowls. Top with a dollop of Szechuan sauce and garnish with remaining onions. Serve at once.

Quick 'n' Easy Risotto

▼

FEEDS 4 IN 20 MINUTES
About 50¢ per serving

All rice-eating cultures have their version of a main dish using rice. The Mexicans have Spanish rice. The Chinese have fried rice. And the Italians have risotto. What these dishes have in common is that they make a main dish of the rice using bits and pieces of leftovers. Each is seasoned according to the lights of its particular culture.

The old Italian method for making risotto, which requires standing and stirring for nearly an hour, would try the patience of most American cooks. I have discovered that you can circumvent this procedure by adopting a method similar to that for making Spanish rice. In short, add boiling broth all at once, slap a lid on, and cook. It isn't very different from most rice procedures.

However, there is one requirement for risotto that you can't get around. You should use medium-grained rice. This rice has a creamier texture and will create the authentic result you want. After cooking, it will have a slightly nutty flavor, and the grains are more moist and tender than those of long-grain rice.

2½ cups chicken broth
1 tablespoon olive oil
1 medium onion, chopped fine
1 clove garlic, pressed
1 cup medium-grain or Arborio rice
⅓ cup Parmesan cheese
½ cup frozen peas

Heat chicken broth to boiling in a medium saucepan.

Meanwhile, in a 10-inch skillet, heat olive oil over medium heat. Add onion and garlic and cook until translucent (about 2 minutes). Then add rice and stir to mix thoroughly. Cook 2–3 minutes. Add boiling chicken broth. Cover, reduce heat, and simmer for exactly 15 minutes. At this point, the broth should be almost absorbed. Remove the lid; cook and stir until the rice looks creamy but not dry. Remove from heat. Now add Parmesan cheese and frozen peas. Stir thoroughly and serve.

Microwave Risotto Primavera

▼

FEEDS 6 IN 30 MINUTES
About 45¢ per serving

Italian women stand patiently at the stove stirring risotto, adding broth or water just drips at a time as the liquid absorbs, until after about an hour, they have a creamy rice dish as comforting as a mother's kiss.

About the only thing an American woman will remain in one place for that long is the birth of her own child. Give us a machine, please. We've got other fish to fry.

You can make risotto easily in the microwave. It's not that it takes a short time, but that it takes very little of yours.

Italians use Arborio rice, which sells for a princely sum in this country. Fortunately, we have cheap alternatives. Good old California medium grain rice, available in every supermarket, stands in quite nicely. Yesterday, I made risotto with some medium-grained sweet rice I'd bought at the Asia Market. That made a lovely, almost translucent rice pudding. It was good and it was cheap.

To finish this, you should just open up the hydrator in the refrigerator and see what you have on hand. I made the risotto last night even though I had just one tomato. Since the recipe calls for 6 tomatoes, I used the one I had and sliced a bunch of radishes in their place. I also didn't have any fresh spinach leaves, but I did have some tired outer leaves from a head of romaine. Chopped, they worked just fine. The idea is to blend rice with fresh vegetables to make a vegetable dish that will taste good, be good for you, and won't cost an arm and a leg.

2 tablespoons olive oil
1 cup medium-grain rice (Arborio is best)
2 green onions, sliced into ½-inch rounds
3 cups chicken broth
6 plum tomatoes, cored and chopped
½ cup fresh spinach leaves (or other greens),
    sliced fine
1 medium carrot, shredded
Salt to taste
Fresh-ground black pepper to taste
Pinch of paprika
Pinch of cayenne
Parmesan cheese for garnish
Parsley for garnish
(continued)

Place oil, uncovered in a deep microwaveable 3-quart casserole dish. Microwave at 100% (HIGH) for 1 minute. Stir in the rice. Microwave uncovered at 100% (HIGH) for 1 minute. Add onion and stir to coat. Microwave at 100% (HIGH) for 3 minutes.

Pour in 2½ cups chicken broth. Microwave uncovered, at 100% (HIGH) for 12 minutes. Pour in remaining broth and tomatoes, spinach leaves, and carrot. Microwave uncovered at 100% (HIGH) for 8 minutes.

Stir in salt and peppers. Cover and let it stand 5–10 minutes. The rice should have absorbed all the liquid now and be a creamy pudding. If not, microwave again at 100% (HIGH) for 2 minutes and let it stand covered a few minutes longer.

Serve topped with a sprinkling of Parmesan and a sprig of parsley.

Spanish Rice

▼

FEEDS 4 IN 30 MINUTES
About 45¢ per serving

This rice dish has been called Spanish by Americans, but it is actually Mexican.

2 tablespoons vegetable oil
1 cup long-grain rice
2 cloves garlic, pressed
1 medium onion, chopped fine
1 16-ounce can stewed tomatoes, plus water to make 2 cups
Chicken, diced (optional)
Peas (optional)

In a 10-inch skillet, heat oil, then add rice. Stirring over medium-high heat, sauté the rice grains until golden. Add garlic and onion and sauté until slightly brown. Add tomatoes with juice and water. Bring to a boil, uncovered. Turn heat to low, cover, and cook 15–20 minutes, without peeking, until all water is absorbed. At the end of the cooking time, toss lightly with a fork and leave rice uncovered. The rice grains will be separate and fluffy.

If you wish to add some bits of finely diced leftover chicken or meat, add it now. Shake a few peas straight from the freezer into the cooked rice; leave the lid on for 5 minutes, and the warmth of the grains will cook the peas.

Basic Fried Rice

▼

FEEDS 4 IN 10 MINUTES
About 65¢ per serving

Chinese fried rice is made with yesterday's leftover boiled rice. This is another way to use small bits and pieces of leftover meat or vegetables. The traditional Chinese choice is roast pork but other meats would do—chicken, shrimp, fish, almost anything except beef. Chinese cooks tell me this dish will not be the same if you simply cook up a pot of rice and begin. The rice should be refrigerated overnight for proper consistency. You can add a few frozen peas right out of the package along with the meat if you wish. The heat of the rice will cook them sufficiently.

3 cups rice, day-old cooked (from 1 cup uncooked)
4 tablespoons salad oil
3 eggs, beaten
Salt and pepper to taste
1 cup roast pork or chicken, diced, or shrimp
  (optional)
Green peas (optional)
1½ teaspoons soy sauce, low-salt
2 green onions, chopped

Wet your hands and break the rice apart. In a 10-inch skillet or wok, heat half the oil over very high heat, then stir-fry rice until heated through (2–3 minutes). Make a well in the center, add remaining oil, then pour in eggs. Season with salt and pepper; scramble. Add meat, peas, soy sauce, and mix all ingredients thoroughly until heated through. Add onions. Press into a bowl. Serve.

Polenta

▼

FEEDS 6 IN 30 MINUTES
About 35¢ per serving

In the South, we call it mush. In Italy, they call it polenta. But any way you name it, cooked and formed cornmeal makes a quick, cheap, and delicious starch dish. You can make it in the microwave with no stirring. At the Santa Fe Bar & Grill in Berkeley, they spike the polenta with bits of fiery red pepper and serve it under grilled fennel sausages. The cost of polenta is so low it's embarrassing, and made in the microwave it's so easy I hate to call it a recipe.

1 cup yellow cornmeal or polenta, uncooked
1 teaspoon salt
4 cups cold water

Optional:
Garlic clove, pressed
Red pepper flakes
Parsley
Basil
Parmesan cheese

That's it. Here's how it goes together: Combine cornmeal and salt with water in a 2-quart microwaveable bowl. Cover with plastic wrap. Place in the microwave and cook at 100% (HIGH) 15 minutes. Let it stand 5 minutes. Then cut in slices. You can serve it as is, with butter and pepper, or you can dribble some spices and cheese in or over it.

Poor Mama's Polenta

▼

FEEDS 8 IN 20 MINUTES
About 39¢ per serving

Now that the USDA has given its blessing to grains, placing them at the base of the nutritional pyramid, we know that the peasants were right all along. Eat more grains. They're good and cheap.

Peasants have always created meals that required more wit and skill than money.

And it is always interesting to me to see how many cooks' tricks translate from culture to culture.

Polenta, for example, a standard in the northern part of Italy, bears a close resemblance to a dish called cornmeal mush. Simply a coarse ground cornmeal, either yellow or white, this basic grain cooked with water until the ground grains swell and lose their raw-as-wallpaper-paste flavor makes a splendid main dish. You can eat polenta with nothing more than butter and Parmesan and a grinding of black peppercorns. You can serve it to children with raisins, brown sugar, and milk. You can cool it in a loaf pan, then slice it and fry it in a little olive oil. You can use polenta in a more complicated casserole type dish: either an Italian style lasagna or a Mexican style tamale pie. Anyway you choose, the good flavor of corn will start your dinner off right.

To this recipe we will add what is called in the panhandle of Texas, cream gravy—nothing more than the skillful blending of flour and fat in a skillet, then whisking in milk until you get a silky smooth thick-as-sour-cream sauce you season to taste with salt and pepper. Properly made, cream gravy is so good you could pour it over shirtboards and people would beg for seconds.

1 cup coarse ground cornmeal
2 teaspoons salt
1 quart water
¼ cup butter or margarine
¼ cup all-purpose flour
2 cups milk
Salt, pepper and cayenne to taste
2 bunches fresh spinach or 20 ounces frozen
4 large eggs, hard-boiled
¾ cup Parmesan cheese, grated

Combine cornmeal, salt and water in a 2 quart microwaveable dish. Microwave at 100% (HIGH) for 12 minutes, stirring once.

To make cream gravy, combine the butter and flour in a cast-iron skillet over medium-high heat. Cook and stir with a fork until the roux is golden and the flour smells aromatic. Then dribble in the milk bit by bit, and cook until the sauce is thick and smooth. Season to taste with salt, pepper, and cayenne. Set aside.

Bring to boil a large pot and a small pot of water. Wash the sand from the spinach, cut off the root ends, then drop the spinach into the boiling water and cook for 1 minute after it regains the boil. Then lift the spinach from the water and refresh under cold running water. Drain and chop.

Preheat the oven to 350° F. Coat a 10x13-inch baking dish with cooking spray and press the cooked polenta into it. Arrange spinach evenly over the polenta. (If using frozen spinach, break it over polenta.) Peel the eggs, cut in half and embed into spinach. Stir about half the Parmesan cheese into the cream gravy, pouring it over the spinach. Sprinkle the remaining Parmesan on top. Bake about 35 minutes until bubbly and brown. Remove to a rack and cool about 15 minutes before cutting into 3-inch squares. Delicious hot or at room temperature.

Marinated Vegetables and Polenta

▼

FEEDS 6 IN 30 MINUTES
About 75¢ per serving

I paid $9.00 a serving for this in a New York restaurant at lunch. You can make this simple vegetarian dish yourself for less than $1.00. Make the polenta ahead of time and add the heated vegetables when ready to eat.

1 Polenta recipe, prepared according to directions on page 35
½ cup Parmesan cheese, grated

Grilled Vegetables:
½ cup olive oil (plus additional to wipe pan and veggies before grilling)
1 whole head garlic
1 large sweet onion
2 bell peppers, one red and one green
1 large egg plant
4 large tomatoes

6 various small squashes—zucchini, yellow crookneck, pattypan
2 cups mushrooms
¼ cup vinegar, red wine or balsamic
2 tablespoons fresh chopped herbs: parsley, basil, chives, thyme
Salt and pepper to taste

Just before you're ready to eat, cut the polenta into thick slices, brush with olive oil and grill. Sprinkle the tops with Parmesan.

Meanwhile, chop all the washed vegetables. Heat oil in a 10-inch skillet over medium-high heat and grill vegetables for 2–3 minutes. Remove from heat. Add vinegar, herbs, and salt and pepper, gently stirring to mix. Allow vegetables to marinate for at least 30 minutes before serving, and can be marinated overnight.

Southwest Couscous Salad

▼

FEEDS 6 IN 20 MINUTES
About 75¢ per serving

Lately, I've been cooking couscous a lot. It's fast, cheap, and tasty. Five minutes in boiling chicken broth, and I've got a dinner base of grain.

Couscous is Moroccan pasta made from the endosperm of durum wheat. Young Marakkech women spend their adolescence learning to hand-roll perfect couscous, thereby offering up this skill in place of a dowry.

Think about teenagers patiently working flour into crushed wheat kernels until they get a crumbly dry mixture that is then steamed over chicken or fish stew, three times—over a period of an hour or so. The result is genuine couscous, a fragrant flavorful grain dish.

1 cup dried couscous
3 tablespoons olive oil, divided
1½ cups chicken broth or lightly salted water
1 medium yellow onion, peeled and finely chopped
2 cloves garlic, finely chopped
1 medium carrot, scraped and finely chopped
1 small jalapeño, seeded and minced (or to taste)

1 teaspoon EACH: ground cumin, coriander, chili powder
1 16-ounce can kidney beans, drained
1 large ripe tomato, finely chopped
¾ cup corn, cooked
¼ cup parsley and/or cilantro leaves
1 cup prepared salsa for dressing

Preheat the oven to 375° F. In a 10-inch oven-proof skillet cook the couscous by first tossing it with 1 tablespoon of oil over medium heat for 2 minutes, then add broth or water and bring to a boil. Stir until all the liquid is absorbed, about 2 minutes. Adjust seasoning with salt, then place the skillet into the oven for 5 minutes. Remove from the oven, fluff the granules with two forks and place in a deep salad bowl. Set aside.

Wipe out the skillet; heat remaining oil over medium-high heat, sautéing onion, garlic, carrot, and jalapeño until they begin to brown. Stir in spices and continue to sauté for 1 minute more.

Stir the kidney beans into the mixture and remove from the heat. Pour mixture into the couscous. Stir in the chopped tomato and corn. Cover and refrigerate until serving time.

Toss with fresh parsley and/or cilantro. Serve with your favorite salsa as a dressing—either tossed with the salad or on the side.

Pear Raisin Kugel

▼

FEEDS 6 IN 30 MINUTES USING
MICROWAVE OR 1 HOUR AND
20 MINUTES USING OVEN
About 25¢ per serving

A kugel is a baked sweet or savory pudding made of noodles, potatoes, or bread. Kugels fall into the category of comfort food, and are a good thing to know how to make. Easy, good and cheap. This dish may be prepared quickly in the microwave, or in a conventional oven.

8 ounces wide egg noodles
3 large eggs
⅓ cup sugar
2 cups low-fat milk
1 teaspoon vanilla
2 tablespoons margarine
½ teaspoon salt
1 teaspoon cinnamon
⅓ cup golden raisins
1 large pear (comice preferred), peeled, cored
*   and chopped*

Spray an 8x8-inch glass baking dish with cooking spray. Preheat oven to 300° F if you plan to bake in a conventional oven.

In a large saucepan bring 4 quarts of water to a boil and cook noodles 4 minutes. Meanwhile, in a medium bowl beat eggs and sugar together until the mixture looks foamy, about 2 minutes. Stir in milk, vanilla, margarine, salt and cinnamon. Pour into baking dish, add raisins and pear. Stir to mix.

Drain noodles and pour into the baking dish over top of mixture. Bake it in the microwave, covered with plastic wrap at 100% (HIGH) 6 minutes. Let stand 5 minutes, then remove the plastic. Alternately, bake in conventional oven, preheated, 1 hour or until browned.

Cut into squares and serve warm or at room temperature.

To fancy up your service, pool easy Rum Raisin Sauce on a dessert plate, then add a square of kugel and top with a fan of fresh-sliced pear. Cut a pear in half and core. Slice thin up to but not including the stem, so that you can fan the pear half out over the kugel square.

Rum Raisin Sauce

▼

MAKES 2 CUPS IN 20 MINUTES
About $1.00 per serving

This sauce keeps in the refrigerator for months. Pour it over vanilla ice cream or plain yellow cake as well as over kugels and other fruits and puddings served for brunch.

1½ cups water
½ cup golden raisins
⅓ cup brown sugar
2 tablespoons butter or margarine
1½ tablespoons cornstarch
2 tablespoons cold water
2 tablespoons rum or 2 teaspoons rum flavoring
(continued)

In a 1-quart microwaveable bowl, combine water with raisins. Microwave at 100% (HIGH) 4 minutes or until the mixture comes to a boil. Set it aside for 10 minutes.

Now stir brown sugar and butter into the raisins, replace in the microwave and cook at 100% (HIGH) 4 minutes, or until the mixture comes to a boil. Meanwhile, dissolve the cornstarch in cold water.

Stir cornstarch solution into the hot sauce. Microwave 45 seconds at 100% (HIGH) or until the mixture thickens. Remove from the microwave and stir in the rum. Cool, pour into a container, cover, and store in the refrigerator until needed.

Tomato/Gravy Pasta

▼

FEEDS 4 IN 20 MINUTES
About 60¢ per serving

The good news is that produce in September is cheap and flavorful. The bad news is that winter's coming and those good, summer vegetables will soon be just a memory. This may be hard to realize when it seems you have more than you know what to do with.

At that time of year, when the tomato vines look desolate but the tomatoes are as good as they're ever going to get, we live on tomato sandwiches for lunch. Thick slabs of tomato grace every dinner plate and tomatoes are chipped into our breakfast omelettes. For us, summer is tomatoes, and we adore them.

Just last night we had an impromptu pasta dish made by chopping a couple of big beefsteak tomatoes, combining them with a couple of matchstick julienned zucchini and a half cup of mixed fresh herbs. We cooked this about 15 minutes in a skillet with a little olive oil, and seasoned it with salt, pepper and a squeeze of fresh lemon juice. We poured this sauce over fresh-cooked pasta and topped it with Parmesan. Dinner in 15 minutes. Good, fresh, cheap.

2 cups chicken gravy
2 cups fresh tomato, chopped
2 cups dry fusilli (or other pasta)
Parmesan cheese for garnish
Fresh-ground pepper

Combine chicken gravy and fresh tomato in a skillet and simmer gently while the pasta cooks. Adjust seasonings with salt and pepper. Meanwhile, cook pasta in boiling, lightly salted water until al dente, up to 15 minutes. Drain pasta and toss with the hot tomato cream sauce.

Serve immediately in soup bowls, with a little Parmesan and fresh pepper sprinkled on top.

Chicken

▼

*T*he humble chicken has been given serious attention by cooks, both Eastern and Western. A good fresh chicken, one with white translucent skin, plump, and with a clean, fresh aroma, can be prepared in innumerable ways with good results.

Chicken is a good choice for company meals for several reasons including economy. But perhaps more important is that poultry does not require precise cooking times. After achieving a basic doneness, there is considerable leeway in the timing of a meal. If the before-dinner conversation is too interesting to interrupt, you can leave a chicken dish for a while longer with no harm done.

In this chapter, I discuss only the two most common poultry products—chicken and turkey. There are other poultry choices you can try, according to what you happen to have available. If you have access to pheasant, you can use any chicken procedure, lengthening cooking times to account for the pheasant's lean flesh. You can also use Cornish hens in chicken recipes—Chicken Pot Roast, in particular. Duck teriyaki is splendid. Quail cacciatore's a natural (cacciatore means "hunter" anyway).

I have arranged these recipes according to the preparation time required, beginning with a recipe using thin-sliced breast meat sautéed in about 10 minutes and working up to an all-day procedure that begins with a frozen chicken. Be sure to read the section **Poaching a Chicken**—for the beginning of that free broth that is used in numerous recipes.

Chicken Comfort

▼

FEEDS 4 IN 20 MINUTES
About 80¢ per serving

In calculating the cost of meat, the foremost consideration is cost per serving rather than cost per pound. Chicken breast, which costs about three times what a whole chicken does, is great in this dish, but thighs yield an even richer flavor. It seems silly to buy boneless chicken pieces, since it takes one quick rip to separate the bones and skin from the meat. You can toss the bones and skin into a pot of water for a batch of free chicken broth to boot.

I have a recipe that was probably originally Oriental—a kind of chicken with plum sauce. Over time, I've pared it down to its rock-bottom potential. In the first place, the original chicken meat was quick-fried in a wok. Well, I hate to clean splattered grease off the stove as much as the next one, so the first thing I tried to do was figure out an alternate plan to frying. The solution to this problem—a very hot oven.

The second problem I have encountered is the availability of plum jam. Maybe I'd have it and maybe I wouldn't. But still, at the end of some long horrendous day when I wanted to get supper over with in about 15 minutes, this recipe came to mind. I discovered that other jams and jellies could stand in place of plum jam quite nicely. It's the sugar that counts in the recipe—it makes a glaze. We have a crabapple tree in our front yard, and once I made a batch of jelly from the first of the crabapples that fell. The truth of it is, those crabapples taste like potatoes and the jelly is merely red and sweet. The kids don't even like it with peanut butter, so I am trying to unload 8 half-pints of crystal-pure but worthless jelly by using it in this recipe. Do you have languishing in your refrigerator some jam or jelly no one will eat? The only kind to avoid is grape, which tends to produce a slate-gray glaze.

In addition to rice, broccoli goes well with this dish. If you stir-fry broccoli in a little oil with 2 garlic buds, then steam it a moment in 2 tablespoons of water, the color and taste combination is serendipity.

3 chicken breast halves or 6 thighs
Half a small onion (about ⅓ cup), minced
1 tablespoon fresh ginger, minced or 1 teaspoon
*   powdered ginger*
1 tablespoon vegetable oil
1 tablespoon soy sauce
1 teaspoon Dijon mustard
Juice and pulp of 1 seeded orange or lemon
½ cup jelly (plum, apricot, crabapple)

Preheat oven to 475° F. Skin and bone the chicken pieces. Using your hands, tear the chicken into nice, bite-sized chunks.

Make a sauce of the remaining ingredients. Thoroughly coat all chicken in sauce. Let stand until oven is fully heated. Now place chicken and sauce in a flat glass dish large enough to hold the pieces without overlapping, and cook uncovered until the chicken is a lovely golden brown (10–12 minutes). Serve over rice.

Kung Pao Chicken

▼

FEEDS 4 IN 30 MINUTES
About 95¢ per serving

2 whole chicken breasts
2 tablespoons reduced-sodium soy sauce
3 tablespoons cornstarch
½ tablespoon hot pepper oil or plain vegetable oil
8 medium dried red peppers
1 green pepper, seeded and cut into large rectangles
1 cup water chestnuts, diced or celery cut on the diagonal into ½-inch pieces
½ cup roasted peanuts
2 green onions, chopped

Seasoning Sauce:
4 tablespoons reduced-sodium soy sauce
2 tablespoons sherry
2 tablespoons red wine vinegar
2 tablespoons sugar
2 teaspoons sesame oil

Bone and skin chicken breasts and cut into about 1-inch pieces. Mix soy sauce and cornstarch into a smooth paste and combine with chicken. Stir to coat all pieces and set aside for 10 minutes. Make the Seasoning Sauce by mixing all of those ingredients in a small bowl. Set aside.

In a wok or large skillet, heat oil over highest setting and fry red peppers until they turn black. (This will run you out of the kitchen as the pepper volatilizes, so throw open all the windows, turn on the exhaust fan, and prepare to stagger out onto the back porch for a breath of fresh air.) Now add chicken pieces and stir-fry for just a few seconds until chicken begins to brown. Add green pepper and water chestnuts or celery and stir-fry until cooked crunchy (no more than 5 minutes total).

Add seasoning sauce and stir until thickened and hot (just a minute or so). Remove from heat, add peanuts and green onions. Mix together and serve—either with rice or noodles.

Chicken Hash

▼

FEEDS 6 IN 30 MINUTES
About 65¢ per serving

If you have poached a chicken in order to use the breast in another recipe, here's what you can do with the rest of the chicken and broth.

1 cup rice, uncooked
2½ cups chicken broth
1 large onion, chopped
2 garlic cloves, minced
2 tablespoons oil or margarine
1 dried red pepper
Salt and pepper to taste
¼–⅓ cup sherry
¼–⅓ cup parsley, chopped
3 cups poached chicken and giblets, diced
1 cup of fresh or frozen green peas or beans (optional)
1 3-ounce jar pimentos
(continued)

Sauce:

1½ tablespoons flour
1½ tablespoons oil
1½ cups chicken stock or ¾ cup stock
¾ cup milk, if you like white gravy
Salt and pepper to taste

Cook rice, covered, in the chicken broth (taste for salt and adjust if needed) over low heat for 20 minutes, or until all broth is absorbed.

In a flameproof 2½-quart casserole, heat oil over medium-high heat and sauté onion and garlic until clear. Add red pepper, salt and pepper to taste, sherry, and parsley. Combine with chicken, stir, and keep over low heat. Add peas or beans if you wish.

Make a roux of flour and oil, then mix with broth (or half broth and half milk), then cook and stir until thick. Stir sauce into rice mixture. Add a small 3-ounce jar of pimentos at the last minute for looks. Adjust salt and pepper as needed. Serve hot.

Quick Chicken Cacciatore

▼

FEEDS 4 IN 1 HOUR 15 MINUTES
About 95¢ per serving

1 3-pound fryer, cut in pieces
4 tablespoons olive oil or other cooking oil
1 medium onion, chopped coarse
1 bell pepper, sliced thin
1 clove garlic, pressed
2 tablespoons minced celery leaves
Pinch of dried or fresh rosemary
Salt and pepper to taste

1 16-ounce can stewed tomatoes or 3 fresh
tomatoes, peeled and chopped
1 tablespoon minced parsley
½ cup dry red wine
1 cup (¼ pound) fresh mushrooms, sliced

In a large roasting pan, heat oil over medium-high heat and brown fryer pieces, a few at a time, on all sides until golden brown (about 15 minutes). While chicken is cooking, cut up vegetables. When chicken is browned, add onion, pepper, garlic, celery, and rosemary. Continue cooking until vegetables begin to brown. Now season with salt and pepper, and add tomatoes, parsley, and red wine. Cover, turn down heat, and simmer until almost tender (about 30 minutes). If juice cooks down, add a little stock or water. Add mushrooms; cover and cook 15–20 minutes more.

Easy Chicken Curry

▼

FEEDS 4 IN 1 HOUR AND 30 MINUTES
About 55¢ per serving

I have found a great way to present a chicken that combines the two criteria which I consider important—easy to make and aesthetically pleasing. Here is a supper dish that takes 10 minutes of actual preparation time. However, it requires splitting a fryer in half. (This is easy to do: just slice through the breast and break the back with your thumbs.)

1 fryer, cut in half
½ cup (¼ pound) margarine
(continued)

1 onion, peeled and minced fine
1 unpeeled apple, cored and minced fine
Juice and pulp of 1 lemon
1 teaspoon (or more) curry powder
1 tablespoon sugar
¼ cup water
Salt and pepper to taste

Preheat oven to 350° F. Lay fryer halves in a greased, flat baking pan or dish. Melt margarine in a small saucepan. Add onion, then apple (these go quick in a processor). Cook and stir over medium-high heat 2 or 3 minutes, then add remaining ingredients and cook 2–3 minutes more. Adjust spices to taste. Pour over chicken, reserving a little for basting. Bake in 350°-F oven until done through (about 1½ hours). Baste occasionally.

Serve with rice cooked in chicken broth. Complementary flavors: peanuts, sliced bananas, yogurt, hard-cooked egg, raisins, almonds, and chopped green onions.

Down South Chicken

▼

FEEDS 4 IN UNDER 2 HOURS
About 70¢ per serving

For a taste of genuine Southern cooking, here's a dish straight from Dixieland that is sure to please any appetite. If you want to take the whole trip to Biloxi, serve with Creole-style okra and hot biscuits.

1 fryer, cut into serving pieces
Salt and pepper to taste

Flour
1 cup vegetable oil
2 heaping tablespoons flour
2 cups hot water
1 stalk celery, chopped
1 large yellow onion, sliced
2 cloves garlic, minced
1 green pepper, cut in julienne strips
1 16-ounce can tomatoes, chopped, with juice
1 cup rice
Salt

Preheat oven to 350° F. Salt and pepper the chicken pieces generously, then dredge in flour. Set aside. In a roaster, heat oil to 350° F. (Any baking pan will do but a turkey roaster that can be used both on top of the stove and in the oven means one less pan to wash.) Fry the chicken at a high temperature, a few pieces at a time, just until barely golden. Remove chicken and reserve on paper towels. Discard all but 2 tablespoons of oil in the roaster. Keep all the pan crumbs. Add an equal amount of flour and stir over medium heat, making a light roux. Pour in the hot water and cook gravy until thick. Salt and pepper to taste. Now place all the vegetables in the gravy, and put the chicken on top, cover, and place in preheated oven. Bake covered until meat falls away from the bone—about 1 hour.

Meanwhile, cook rice according to package directions. When the chicken is cooked, remove to a warmed platter. Add the rice to the gravy, mix well, and mound the rice and vegetables around the chicken on the platter and serve.

Now isn't that the most Southern dish you've ever heard of?

Chicken Pot Roast

▼

FEEDS 6 IN 2–2½ HOURS
About 95¢ per serving

You can count on the French to take something as commonplace as Mother's pot roast, substitute a chicken, use their French method on it, and come up with a delicious company dish. This is a wonderful recipe for Cornish game hens.

4 tablespoons butter or margarine
1 clove garlic, minced
½ teaspoon thyme
Juice of ½ lemon
1 3-pound roasting chicken
½ pound salt pork or bacon ends
6 carrots, peeled and cut into chunks
6 small potatoes, scrubbed
2 medium onions, peeled and sliced thin
Salt and pepper to taste

Preheat oven to 350° F. Mash together butter, garlic, thyme, and lemon juice; rub half of this paste into chicken cavity and set aside the rest. Blanch pork by boiling in small pan of water for 2 minutes. Drain and dice fine. Brown diced pork in a roaster, then remove from grease with slotted spoon. Brown chicken in pork fat, slowly, on all sides until it is an even golden color (about 25 minutes).

Meanwhile, in a skillet melt remaining butter mixture and sauté carrots, potatoes, and onions over medium-low heat, stirring from time to time. When chicken is golden, remove from roaster. Drain all but 1 tablespoon of the oil from the roaster, then return the cooked pork and the chicken to the roaster and fill in the open spaces with the browned vegetables and juice. Salt and pepper well. Cover tightly and cook in preheated oven for about 1½ hours or until leg joint moves freely. Baste frequently.

Elysee's Oriental Chicken

▼

FEEDS 4 IN 3½ HOURS
(INCLUDES MARINATING TIME)
About 80¢ per serving

Wings or thighs work equally well.

2 pounds chicken wings or thighs

Marinade:
½ cup reduced-sodium soy sauce
1 tablespoon brown sugar
½ teaspoon dry mustard
¼ cup cooking oil
¼ cup orange juice
1 tablespoon lemon juice

Place chicken in a covered 10x13-inch Pyrex dish. Combine marinade ingredients and pour over the chicken; marinate 2 hours or so. Turn occasionally.

In a 350°-F oven, cook chicken in marinade, uncovered, for about 1 hour or until done. Turn every 10–15 minutes. When cooked, the chicken will have a delicious golden glaze and the marinade will have evaporated from the dish. During the last 5 minutes of cooking time, garnish the chicken with thin slices of fresh orange rind. Serve with rice and stir-fried vegetables.

POACHING A CHICKEN

When Grandma killed the old red rooster, she had to boil it all day long—it was a wily yardbird. But the chicken that comes to your kitchen lived a short uneventful life in a cage with lights blaring and sometimes Muzak to eat by, so it scarcely had the muscle tone to walk.

You don't need to boil a chicken anymore. Here is a way to cook chicken meat so that it will be tender, delicious, flavorful—not overcooked, stringy, dry, or rubbery.

Place a whole chicken in a big pot. Cover well with cold water; don't salt. Bring the water to a full rolling boil, reduce heat, cover, and simmer for 20 minutes. Turn heat off and allow to stand, covered, until cooled to room temperature.

Remove bird from the broth, skin, and debone. Now you have the chicken meat with all its flavor intact, without having boiled away half its nutrients. And it was no more trouble than boiling it all day.

GREAT CHICKEN BROTH

Replace the carcass in the broth, breaking up larger bones; add the skin and neck. If you wish, you can add carrot, celery, and onion. Let broth simmer uncovered an hour or so. Now salt to taste. By now the broth should be rich, flavorful, aromatic. Strain broth and freeze in about 1- or 2-cup portions for use in other recipes.

Ginger Chicken

▼

FEEDS 6 IN 2 HOURS
About 95¢ per serving

1 3-pound frying chicken, cut in pieces
¼ cup peanut oil or other vegetable oil
6 green onions and tops, sliced thin
½ cup fresh ginger root, grated
4 tablespoons reduced-sodium soy sauce
2 tablespoons dry sherry
4 tablespoons sugar

Poach chicken following directions on this page. When cooled, drain chicken, skin, and debone; return skin to stock. Tear the chicken into bite-sized pieces. Arrange in a shallow 10x13-inch baking dish.

In a skillet, heat oil; sauté onions and ginger over medium-high heat for about 30 seconds. Remove from skillet and sprinkle over chicken. To the same skillet, add remaining ingredients. Boil briefly, then pour over chicken. Cover and let marinate at room temperature about 1 hour. Serve at room temperature with rice and a good green salad.

Chinese Chicken Salad

▼

FEEDS 4 IN 15 MINUTES
About $1.00 per serving

This recipe requires a whole cooked chicken. It is more economical to buy a chicken and roast it yourself in advance, but if you're in a hurry you can buy one on the way home from work. Just stop by the delicatessen, pick up a warm roaster chicken, a head of iceberg lettuce, and a bunch of fresh cilantro, and you'll have the dinner prepared in less time than it takes to heat up the stove. This dish consists of a combination that is always a pleasant surprise—cold greens and warm chicken. Tom and Kathy, the couple who invented this dish, keep going on diets because they love to eat too well, and they point out that this dish is really low in calories.

The sesame oil and hot oil called for in these recipes are both found in the Chinese section of the grocery store. Although they cost about a dollar a bottle, they have been in my cabinet forever. The bottle of hot oil, which looks like a small Worcestershire bottle, is practically a lifetime supply because I use only two or three drops at a time. The sesame oil—which is simply splendid on any stir-fried vegetable—is in a bottle so sticky and dust-soaked that if anyone saw it, they'd probably refuse to eat what came out of it. But these long-term investments in the kitchen are worth the money. They are stable if properly stored in a cool, dark, dry place. They can provide a subtle underpinning to a vast number of dishes.

I buy sesame seed in bulk at a co-op grocery store where it costs about a dollar a pound—which goes a long way. If sesame seeds are available to you only in small spice bottles, just leave them out. They're too expensive except in bulk.

1 2-pound whole small roasted chicken
1 head iceberg lettuce
1 cup fresh cilantro leaves
¼ cup sesame seeds
1 tablespoon sesame oil
Few drops hot pepper oil
1 tablespoon wine vinegar

Bone chicken and cut meat into julienne strips. Set meat aside and keep warm. Shred lettuce very fine. Combine with cilantro leaves and sesame seeds. (You can toast the sesame seeds if you like.) Toss with oils and vinegar. Mix with chicken. Serve.

TOASTING SESAME SEEDS
To toast sesame seeds, spread one layer deep in a hot, dry skillet, and cook over high heat until golden, about 2 minutes. Quickly transfer to another dish; otherwise they will burn.

Acapulco Enchiladas

▼

FEEDS 6 IN 1 HOUR
About 90¢ per serving

Sauce:
4 tablespoons vegetable oil
4 large yellow onions, chopped coarse
1 15-ounce can tomato sauce plus a can of water
1 8-ounce can tomato sauce plus a can of water
Salt and pepper to taste

Chicken Filling:
1 whole poached chicken breast or 4 thighs
1 6½-ounce can chopped green chiles
1 tablespoon sour cream or yogurt
18 fresh corn tortillas
1 tablespoon oil
8 ounces longhorn or cheddar cheese, grated

In a large Dutch oven, heat oil over medium-low heat and sauté onions until limp and transparent (25 minutes). Add tomato sauce and water, and salt and pepper, simmering over low heat to a catsuplike consistency. Keep hot for assembling the enchiladas.

Meanwhile, make the filling combining chicken, green chiles, and sour cream.

Preheat oven to 400° F. Grease a 10x13-inch glass baking dish. Heat remaining oil in a 7-inch skillet and with tongs, dip tortillas into oil for 15 seconds, then into the hot tomato sauce for 30 seconds. Place in baking dish. After you have dipped all tortillas, stuff with chicken stuffing, roll tightly, and place flap side down. Pour remaining sauce over the enchiladas, cover with grated cheese, and bake until cheese bubbles and browns (about 10 minutes). Serve hot.

Honey Mustard Chicken

▼

FEEDS 4 IN 45 MINUTES
About $1.00 per serving

This easy supper entrée is quick to prepare. Serve with rice and a green salad.

¼ cup ball-park style yellow mustard
3 tablespoons honey
Juice and zest of half a lemon
1 pound boneless, skinless chicken thighs
⅔ cup bread crumbs
Salt and pepper to taste
1 tablespoon canola or other vegetable oil

Preheat oven to 375° F. Coat an 8x8-inch glass baking dish with cooking spray. Combine mustard, honey, and lemon juice in a small bowl. Place bread crumbs on a piece of waxed paper. Salt and pepper to taste. Dip chicken pieces first into mustard mixture, then in bread crumbs. Salt and pepper to taste. Place in the baking dish, sides not touching. Drizzle evenly with oil. Bake uncovered 30–35 minutes or until golden brown and cooked through.

Braised Chicken in Tomato Sauce

▼

FEEDS 4 IN 1 HOUR
About $1.00 per serving

Here's your chance to try your hand at substitution. This dish is so easy you'll soon be able to do it without looking at the recipe. Substitute fresh tomatoes from the garden—just chop up a handful—and the dish will sing. Open a little can of tomato paste, thin it with water and use that. Try a jolt of tomato catsup if that's all you've got.

The basic idea is to brown a chicken in oil with onion, garlic and herbs, then braise it in a rich tomato sauce.

1 3-pound chicken, cut into serving pieces
Salt and pepper to taste
2 tablespoons olive or vegetable oil
1 large yellow onion, coarsely chopped
2 cloves garlic, peeled and chopped
½ teaspoon EACH dried oregano and dried basil
  leaves
½ teaspoon sugar
¼–½ cup water
1 16-ounce can tomato sauce

Pull any loose fat off the chicken and discard. Salt and pepper the pieces generously. In a large stewpot, heat the oil, then brown the chicken on all sides, turning the pieces from time to time until golden (about 15 minutes). While the chicken is browning, add the onion, garlic, and the herbs, browning them along with the bird. Sprinkle sugar over the onions about half way through. Stir and move everything around in the skillet, turning the bird and scraping up the brown bits that cling to the bottom of the pan. Add a little water, scraping it until it's almost evaporated and a golden brown liquid bubbles.

Then pour the tomato sauce over the bird, lower the temperature to simmer, cover, and cook until the chicken is done and the sauce is a catsuplike consistency (about 45 minutes). Add tablespoons of water as needed to keep from cooking dry. Turn the chicken pieces occasionally.

Serve the chicken and sauce over rice or pasta. Garnish each serving with a sprig of parsley if you've got it.

Vegetarian Entrées

▼

The most remarkable change in American supermarkets in the last ten years has taken place in the produce section. If you think about the simple square footage now given over to fresh fruits and vegetables, not to mention the increase in variety of items, you will recognize that Americans have changed their shopping and eating habits.

Good fresh vegetables and fruits are the best bargains available. By shopping for fresh produce in season, when the harvest delivers the best quality for the lowest cost, you can provide an enormous variety of dishes during the year. The grocery store where I shop is large and busy. I can usually tell what the best produce buys are just by looking to see where the carts are clustered. If I have to jockey for position, I know there's something good that day.

Besides saving money, vegetable meals are always a healthy choice. An artichoke, for example, only has 25 calories, yet provides bounteous quantities of fiber, potassium, calcium, and iron. A hefty half-pound serving of asparagus at 48 calories offers calcium, phosphorus and potassium. Well, OK, so a half-pound avocado does have 457 calories and 41 grams of unsaturated fats; it also offers calcium, fiber and protein. And besides, it tastes so good.

For the once-a-week vegetarian meal that I prepare for our family, I just pick up whatever looks good, then figure out what to do with it once I get it home. There are other places in this book where you can find primarily vegetarian entrées as well (see Soups and Pasta and Rice).

If you find a spectacular bargain—some sumptuous, fresh, and extraordinarily cheap vegetable—you can make a meal on it alone. One day I found fresh asparagus at a roadside stand at a giveaway price. It was at its peak of perfection. For supper that night, all we had was asparagus—mountains of steamed asparagus with a little hollandaise—and a loaf of hot sourdough bread.

Lowfat Parmigiana

▼

FEEDS 6 IN 1 HOUR 30 MINUTES
About 75¢ per serving

This recipe comes from one of those loud New York Italian families so passionate about food they fairly weep over a good meal. When they start cooking, you'd better stand out of the way and just wait for the best Italian food you ever ate.

2 medium eggplants
Salt to taste
Olive oil cooking spray

Sauce:
2 tablespoons olive oil
1 onion, peeled and sliced thin
4 cloves garlic, minced
½ bell pepper, seeded and chopped coarse
2 cups (½ pound) fresh mushrooms, sliced thin
1 medium zucchini, scrubbed and sliced into
  rounds
3 medium tomatoes, chopped or 1 15-ounce
  can with juice)
1 6-ounce can tomato paste plus 1 can water
1 8-ounce can tomato sauce plus 1 can water
1 teaspoon sugar
¾ cup vermouth
1 tablespoon soy sauce
Salt to taste
1 tablespoon fresh basil or 1 teaspoon dried
2 tablespoons oregano or 1 tablespoon dried

Cheese Topping:
(¼ pound) lowfat mozzarella cheese, grated
(¼ pound) lowfat jack cheese, grated
½ cup Parmesan cheese, grated

Cut eggplants into thin slices, salt well, and let stand in a colander for 20 minutes to draw out juices. Then rinse under cold running water and blot dry.

Meanwhile, make the sauce. Pour 2 tablespoons of oil into a large saucepan, and sauté onions over medium-high heat until translucent. Add remaining vegetables in order from the list, cooking and stirring 2–3 minutes after each addition. Then add remaining ingredients. Reduce heat and let simmer for 30 minutes or so.

Grate cheeses and set aside.

Preheat broiler and spray a baking sheet with cooking spray. Carefully arrange dry eggplant slices one layer deep on the baking sheet. Spritz with cooking spray and broil until brown, about 6 minutes.

By the time you have broiled all the eggplant, the sauce will be ready and you can begin assembling the dish. Preheat oven to 350° F. Spritz a large, shallow baking dish with cooking spray, then alternate layers of eggplant and sauce until you have filled the dish ¾ full. Top with cheese mixture. Bake uncovered until cheese is bubbly and brown, about 20 minutes.

Make a good salad to go with this by cutting raw zucchini rings into a bowl and topping with a dressing combining a tablespoon of fresh basil and olive oil (see **Basic Marinara Sauce** for frozen cubes), with a tablespoon of fresh oregano and olive oil. For dessert, fresh (continued) applesauce and vanilla ice cream make a great combination. Not quite gelato, but Italian enough to pass. Fellini would have loved it.

Eggplant Curry

▼

FEEDS 4 IN ABOUT 40 MINUTES
About 50¢ per serving

When choosing the eggplant for this dish, find one with a dark satin purple-black color. Decline any with soft or brown spots. Large, heavy eggplants can be bitter and contain more seeds, so choose a medium-sized one that feels light for its size.

Using Basmati rice for this dish will take you a step out of the ordinary, but it costs a little more.

1 cup rice, uncooked—Basmati is the best
1 eggplant (about 1 pound), unpeeled, chopped
3 tablespoons butter or margarine
½ teaspoon cumin seed
1 teaspoon salt
1 teaspoon turmeric
1 teaspoon cayenne or red pepper
1 onion, chopped coarse
2 cups water
1 large ripe tomato, chopped coarse
1 cup yogurt or ½ cup buttermilk

Cook rice in a medium saucepan according to package directions. Chop eggplant, salt well, and place in a colander to draw out unwanted juices.

In a 10-inch skillet, heat butter and stir in spices. Cook 1 minute. Add onion and sauté until limp. Rinse the eggplant, pat dry, and add to skillet. Stir, coating eggplant well (you may have to add a little more butter at this point). Add water and tomato. Cover and cook eggplant thoroughly (at least 25 minutes). Remove cover, raise heat, then stir and boil hard to reduce liquid until you have a thick vegetable mixture. Stir in yogurt and heat but do not boil. Serve immediately over rice.

You can garnish with raisins, diced hard-boiled eggs, green onions, crushed peanuts, chutney, crumbled bacon, or cucumbers in yogurt.

Vo Bacon's Moussaka

▼

FEEDS 8–10 IN 2 HOURS
About 65¢ per serving

Vo Bacon is an American food writer who has lived in Australia for the past thirty years. Author of several cookbooks, she has a deft hand with a moussaka. Her recipe produces the lightest, most delicate version I have ever tried. She uses New Zealand ground beef, which is quite lean and free of chemical additives—similar to what used to be raised in this country as range beef. If you are using standard-grade hamburger in the recipe, you should alter the procedure by browning the meat in a dry skillet, then draining it, and combining it with the sautéed onions.

This recipe easily feeds 8 people, 10 if they're not too ravenous. You could halve the recipe for a smaller group, but the time and work is the same whether you're cooking for 4 or 8. Considering that the dish is even better the second day, you might want to go ahead and cook the whole thing, even if you plan to feed only 4.

2 large eggplants, unpeeled, sliced 1-inch thick
Salt to taste
Paprika for garnish
Cooking oil spray

Sauce:
1 tablespoon olive oil
2 large onions, chopped fine
1 clove garlic, pressed
14 ½ ounces beef consommé or homemade beef
    broth
16 ounces stewed tomatoes
6 ounces tomato paste
2 teaspoons basil
1 teaspoon cinnamon
½ teaspoon oregano
Salt to taste
⅓ cup dry red wine

Topping:
1 cup lowfat cheddar cheese, grated
1 tablespoon flour
1 cup light sour cream
1 cup dry cottage cheese

Preheat broiler. Salt both sides of eggplant slices. Let stand in a colander to draw out juices (20–30 minutes). Rinse salt off under running water, then dry slices thoroughly. Sprinkle with paprika. Spritz with cooking spray. Spritz a baking sheet and arrange slices one layer deep. Broil until golden brown, about 6 minutes. Reserve.

Meanwhile, heat oil in a 10-inch skillet and sauté the onions and garlic. Add beef stock. Simmer until onions are tender (5 minutes). Then add remaining ingredients except wine. Salt to taste. Simmer covered for 30 minutes. Remove lid, add wine, and simmer uncovered until thick. Set aside.

Meanwhile, in a medium-sized bowl, toss grated cheese with flour, then combine with sour cream and cottage cheese. Stir to mix thoroughly.

Preheat oven to 350° F. Using a large casserole, lasagna pan, or two medium casseroles (a rectangular cake pan is too shallow), place a little sauce in bottom of casserole. Alternate eggplant and sauce until pan is ⅔ filled. Cover with sour cream topping.

Bake uncovered for about 50 minutes or until golden brown and bubbly on top. Let cool at least 15 minutes before cutting. Serve with a simple green salad, maybe some sautéed yellow squash rings or whole green beans, and a loaf of French bread. Wonderful.

Onion Pie

▼

FEEDS 4 IN 1 HOUR 30 MINUTES
About 45¢ per serving

1 prepared and baked 9-inch pie crust
4 yellow onions, sliced thin
2 tablespoons cooking oil
Salt and pepper to taste
1 teaspoon sugar
1 tablespoon flour
2 eggs
2 tablespoons milk or cream
Sprinkle of paprika
3 ounces provolone cheese, sliced thin

In a 10-inch skillet over medium-low heat, brown onion in oil (15–20 minutes). Keep covered, and turn from time to time. Watch closely to make sure they don't burn. About ⅔ of the way through the cooking, season to taste with salt and pepper and sprinkle with sugar to enhance the glaze.

When onions are thoroughly reduced and brown, sprinkle with flour, cook, and stir to make a golden roux.

Preheat oven to 350° F. Pour onions into baked crust. Beat eggs and milk. Pour over onions. Sprinkle with paprika. Cover with provolone. Bake uncovered until custard sets (45 minutes) and a knife inserted in the center comes out clean.

Pumpkin Provençal

▼

FEEDS 4 IN 45 MINUTES
About 50¢ per serving

Pumpkins are a good source of Vitamin A, low in calories, and dirt cheap by the pound.

2 tablespoons olive oil
3 cups raw pumpkin, cut into cubes
1 onion, chopped coarse
1 garlic clove, sliced thin
1 cup (¼ pound) fresh mushrooms, sliced
Salt and pepper to taste
6 ounces tomato sauce
⅔ cup Parmesan cheese, grated

Preheat oven to 350° F. In a 10-inch skillet, heat oil over medium-high heat, then sauté pumpkin cubes, onion, garlic, and mushrooms until they are beginning to brown. Salt and pepper to taste.

When cooked, remove from heat, stir in tomato sauce and half the cheese and mix well. Pour into a well-greased 1-quart casserole dish, top with remaining cheese, and bake uncovered for 25 minutes.

SPAGHETTI SQUASH

You can use spaghetti squash in any recipe that calls for regular spaghetti. The spaghetti squash is a lovely golden color, has a typical squash taste, and is almost free of calories. Its big advantage is that you can cook it hours before you are ready to serve. It will not turn to glue like wheat spaghetti does.

To precook the spaghetti squash, simply place it whole on a rack in a large roaster with 1 inch of water, cover, and steam for 30 minutes. Remove and let it cool down until it won't burn your hands. Cut in 2 pieces. Using a spoon, carefully remove seeds and inner membrane, taking care not to cut into the flesh of the squash.

Using the same spoon, begin digging flesh away from the cavity. It will peel off like long, golden strands of spaghetti. Simply reserve in a bowl until you have made the sauce you planned to use. It's good with marinara as well as with eggplant and mushroom. You can even invent something to go over the squash.

Kids are fascinated by the operation of getting the squash out of its skin.

Tomato Vegetable Sauce

▼

FEEDS 4 IN 30 MINUTES
About 45¢ per serving

Although there may be some who shun meat for philosophical reasons, many eat vegetarian dishes for economical reasons.

This basic sauce is good over spaghetti and rice. It's great over spaghetti squash. It is good by itself in a soup bowl as a vegetable side dish. It is good with Parmesan cheese. It's just plain good.

1 large eggplant or 1½ pounds zucchini, unpeeled, cut into big chunks
1 28-ounce can stewed tomatoes
10–15 leaves of fresh basil or 2 tablespoons dried basil
5–10 leaves of fresh oregano or 1 teaspoon dried oregano
1 clove garlic, sliced thin
1 tablespoon sugar
Salt and pepper to taste

Cut eggplant or zucchini into large chunks, salt well, and set aside in a colander to draw out juices.

In a medium-sized saucepan, break up tomatoes with a spoon. Bring tomatoes to a gentle boil, adding remaining ingredients. Simmer uncovered for 10 minutes, tasting and adjusting seasonings.

Rinse eggplant or zucchini and pat dry, add
(continued)

to tomato sauce, cover, and simmer until eggplant is thoroughly cooked but still holding its shape—about 20 minutes.

Eat the sauce as it is or with a shake of Parmesan cheese on it, or on rice, spaghetti, or spaghetti squash. Looks delicious and tastes even better.

Vegetable Chalupa
▼
FEEDS ANY NUMBER IN 15 MINUTES
About 50¢ per serving

If you are feeding 4, using one each of the vegetables and around 1 cup of mushrooms will allow for generous servings. You can feed 8 or 12 or 20 with this offering for a buffet. Offer a side of refried beans. Spanish rice. Crisp tortillas. Mexican beer. Can't you see the party building?

Zucchini, sliced in rounds
Onion, chopped coarse
Mushrooms, cut vertically
Celery, cut horizontally
Olive oil
Salt to taste
Corn tortillas
Sour cream or yogurt
Fresh ripe tomatoes, chopped
Cheddar cheese, grated
Very ripe avocado, sliced
Picante sauce

Braise equal amounts zucchini, onion, mushrooms, and celery in small amount of olive oil until onion is clear. Salt to taste. Meanwhile, heat tortillas in a small dry skillet about 15 seconds per side. Put each tortilla on a warmed dinner plate. Pile on the braised vegetables and cheese. Run under the broiler until bubbly. Then top with a dollop of sour cream or yogurt, tomatoes, and avocado. Salt as needed. Serve with picante sauce.

Calabasitas
▼
FEEDS 4 IN 20 MINUTES
About 60¢ per serving

1 tablespoon margarine or vegetable oil
2 bell peppers, seeded and cut into julienne strips
4 small zucchini, cut into julienne strips
¼ pound fresh mushrooms, sliced lengthwise
Pinch of salt
4 green onions, chopped
2 cups Swiss cheese (about ¼ pound), grated
1 tablespoon chili powder
1 ripe avocado, peeled, pitted, and cut into julienne strips

In a 10-inch skillet, heat oil over medium-high heat. Sauté in oil the peppers, zucchini, and mushrooms just until crisp and beginning to brown. Don't overdo it. Salt to taste.

Meanwhile, in a medium serving bowl, combine onions with half the Swiss cheese. Add chili powder. Stir to mix thoroughly. Then add sautéed vegetables. Toss and top with remaining Swiss cheese. Garnish with avocado slices. Good with crisp tortillas.

Zucchini Frittata

▼

This frittata does not look like a quiche. It is thin and golden brown on top and bottom. It is just as good at room temperature as it is hot. For a party you could cut it into bite-sized squares and serve on toothpicks. Great with French bread.

1 cup zucchini, grated
½ teaspoon salt
½ slice of bread, torn into bits or crumbed in
    the food processor
3 tablespoons milk
4 tablespoons Parmesan cheese, grated
¼ teaspoon fresh lemon peel, grated
¼ teaspoon salt
Pinch of sugar
4 eggs
2 tablespoons butter or margarine
2 or 3 green onions
¼ cup fresh parsley, chopped

Blanch grated zucchini one of two ways. You can place the lightly salted zucchini in a covered glass dish and microwave it on high for 2 minutes, or you can blanch it in a small pan of boiling salted water for 3 minutes. Use either method, then drain it in a colander.

While the zucchini is blanching, soak bread crumbs in a medium bowl with milk, adding cheese, lemon peel, salt, and sugar; set aside. Beat the eggs in a medium-sized bowl until lemony and thick, then combine with bread mixture. Melt butter in a 10-inch ovenproof skillet and sauté onions and parsley until soft.

Stir zucchini into bread mixture and pour into skillet. Cook over medium-low heat until eggs are firm but still slightly moist. Then slide skillet under the broiler to brown the top lightly (about 5 minutes). Slice in pie wedges and serve.

Cazuelo Sabrosa

▼

Here's a vegetarian casserole to feed the family or to take to a potluck.

1 tablespoon olive oil
1 medium onion, cut into thin slices
6 cloves garlic, minced
2 ribs celery, cut into bite-sized pieces
1 medium green pepper, seeded and chopped
1 fresh jalapeño, seeded and chopped (optional)
16 ounces red kidney beans, drained
2 cups corn, fresh, frozen or canned, drained
2 cups tomato, fresh or 16 ounces canned,
    chopped with juice
4½ ounces diced green chiles
1 cup black olives, drained
(Continued)

1 cup rigatoni or macaroni, uncooked
1 tablespoon chili powder
Salt and pepper to taste
1 cup plain nonfat yogurt or buttermilk
2 cups (5 ounces) jack cheese, grated
Fresh cilantro leaves

Preheat oven to 350° F. Heat oil in large skillet over medium-high heat. Sauté onion, garlic, and peppers until the onions begin to brown. Stir in beans, corn, tomatoes, black olives, green chiles, uncooked pasta, chili powder, salt and pepper to taste and yogurt. Pour into a 13x9x2½-inch baking dish. Top with cheese, cover, and bake 45 minutes or until the pasta is done and the liquid is absorbed. Remove the cover and let it stand a few minutes before serving. Garnish each serving with cilantro.

Zuke Bars

▼

FEEDS 6 IN 1 HOUR
About 60¢ per serving

Combine a big squash with savory fillings, you'll get a succulent late summer dinner. Feel free to substitute enormous pattypan squashes, or small pumpkins for the big zuke. You can, of course, divide the filling among single serving size squashes and make a handsome plate of this one-dish dinner.

1 3–4-pound zucchini
2 tablespoons olive oil
1 large yellow onion, coarsely chopped
6 cloves garlic, finely chopped

¾ pound ground turkey
2 cups chopped plum tomatoes, fresh or canned
2 cups bread crumbs
½ cup Italian parsley, finely chopped
1 teaspoon dried oregano
Salt and freshly milled black and red pepper to taste
¾ cup Parmesan cheese, freshly grated

Preheat the oven to 350° F. Cut the squash in half lengthwise. Scoop out the seeds and pith, leaving a ½-inch thick shell. Place the squash halves on a cookie sheet and par-bake while preparing the filling, about 20 minutes.

In a large skillet, heat the olive oil over medium-high heat, then sauté the onion and garlic until beginning to brown. Crumble in the ground turkey and continue cooking until the turkey has lost its pink cast.

Stir in the tomatoes, turn the heat down to medium and simmer until the tomatoes are tender and the liquid is almost evaporated, about 15 minutes. Remove from the heat and stir in the remaining ingredients, except cheese.

Remove the squash from the oven and pat out any juices from the cavity with a paper towel. Scoop the filling into the squash halves, top with cheese, and place it back into the preheated oven for 30 minutes. Remove from the oven and let stand 5 minutes before serving. Slice thick for each serving.

Roasted Root Vegetables

▼

FEEDS 6 IN ABOUT 1 HOUR 15 MINUTES
About 40¢ per serving

Serve these vegetables along with couscous for a heartwarming winter dinner. Easy on the heart and the pocketbook.

*1 medium rutabaga, peeled and cut into big
    chunks*
*1 medium turnip, peeled and cut into big
    chunks*
*1 large russet potato, peeled and cut into big
    chunks*
*1 large parsnip, peeled and split in half verti-
    cally, then cut into 2-inch pieces*
*1 large carrot, peeled, split in half vertically,
    then cut into 2-inch pieces*
3 small red beets, peeled
1 large yellow onion, peeled and quartered
¼ cup olive oil
2 tablespoons fresh rosemary needles
Salt and pepper to taste
¼ teaspoon sugar
1 cup chicken broth
Rosemary sprigs for garnish

Preheat the oven to 375° F. Meanwhile, place cut veggies in a large, open roasting pan. Pour oil over and toss to coat each vegetable thoroughly.

Season the vegetables with rosemary, salt and pepper, and sugar. Toss to coat. Pour in the chicken broth. Place in the oven and roast until tender and golden brown, about 1 hour. Turn veggies from time to time. If the liquid boils away, add a few spoons full of broth or water to prevent the vegetables from sticking to the pan. Serve with sprigs of fresh rosemary to garnish.

FAST CORN ON THE COB
Our favorite way to cook corn on the cob is to microwave an ear—laid in the microwave as it comes, in the shuck—for four minutes at 100% (HIGH). Whack off both ends of the cob, peel the shucks, string the silks, then cut the corn from the cob.

Lettuce and Pea Chiffonade

▼

FEEDS 2 IN 10 MINUTES
About 40¢ per serving

10 outer leaves of iceberg (or other) lettuce
1 medium onion, finely chopped
1 cup frozen peas
1 tablespoon butter or margarine
½ teaspoon sugar
Salt and pepper to taste
1 tablespoon milk or cream

Heat butter in a 10-inch skillet over medium-high heat. Meanwhile, to make chiffonade, stack the lettuce leaves then roll into a fat green cigar. Using a French chef's knife, rock the knife back and forth, cutting the lettuce into fine, even shreds.

Sauté lettuce and onions, stirring, until the lettuce is limp and the onion is translucent. (continued)

Add peas. Cook and stir a moment. Season with sugar, salt and pepper. Stir a minute, then add milk. Stir and cook 30 seconds longer. Divide between 2 plates.

Aromatic Stuffed Artichokes

▼

FEEDS 4 IN 90 MINUTES
About 90¢ per serving

This artichoke recipe has much to recommend it. In the first place, it will give you an alternative to serving artichokes dipped in hollandaise or lemon butter—divine in taste, but devilishly fat-filled. Garlic perfume will permeate the leaves, and the taste of parsley and mint are bright and fresh.

For me this dish is really cheap because I make bread, always have old ends lying about, and I grow parsley and mint out in the backyard. If you don't have these homegrown luxuries, use good-quality heels of bought bread and dried herbs.

When buying artichokes, choose large ones that are heavy for their size, with leaves that cling tightly to the globe. Don't hesitate to buy one with bronze-tinged leaves. That's just a kiss of frost and will not harm the quality of the thistle. Don't buy dry-looking artichokes with splayed leaves.

4 large globe artichokes
Juice and zest of 1 lemon
4 heels and slices of whole wheat bread
½ cup fresh parsley, finely chopped, or 4 tablespoons dried
¼ cup fresh mint leaves, finely chopped, or 2 tablespoons dried
3 cloves garlic, finely sliced
¼ cup olive oil, divided
⅔ cup Parmesan cheese, grated

Cut the stalk off each artichoke. Then, using a sharp butcher knife, cut off the top ¼ of each artichoke. Squeeze lemon juice into a bowl; scrape zest into the juice. Rub the lemon halves against the cut edges of the artichokes.

Stand the artichokes, bottoms down, in a steamer. Place the steamer inside a skillet or large pan. Add 1 inch of water to the pan, cover, and steam the artichokes until tender, 30–45 minutes. Remove the lid from the steamer and cool the artichokes a few minutes so you can handle them.

Meanwhile, preheat the oven to 350° F. Tear bread into small pieces and crumbs. Toss the bread with parsley, mint, and garlic. Withhold 1 tablespoon of oil, then drizzle the rest of it into the mixture. Add lemon juice and zest and toss to coat. Finally, stir in the Parmesan.

Gently open the leaves of each artichoke and stuff the openings with the parsley bread stuffing. Coat the tops of the leaves with the remaining tablespoon of oil. Place the artichokes in a baking dish just large enough to hold them comfortably, one layer deep. Pour ¼ cup water into the dish. Bake uncovered in the preheated oven just until the bread looks toasty, about 20–25 minutes.

Serve hot or at room temperature. May be made several hours before serving and held at room temperature, covered.

SUPPER CAKES

I always figure if you can pick a dish for supper that's quick and easy to do, can be made without a trip to the store, and that will leave the folks at the table feeling satisfied, you've succeeded at making a good and cheap dinner.

A vegetable cake recipe is versatile. Whether you call them pancakes or fritters, quickly stirred-together cakes that are laden with vegetables, then griddle baked make a fast and satisfying supper. Make them when you're tired, when you're hungry, and when you don't want to spend too much money or time getting the dinner together.

This recipe is golden-colored from the egg and cornmeal, flecked with green from the cilantro, and crunchy with the addition of any of a number of starchy vegetables that you may find in your refrigerator.

In the summer, I make these cakes using the endless squashes we seem to fall heir to. In the winter, I may use bits and pieces of vegetables that seem to languish in the hydrator tray: turnip, eggplant, the common potato, all make delicious vegetable cakes and can be used singly or in combination.

How you top the cakes is also a matter of personal preference. Around our house, we figure anything topped with salsa is supper. We like our dinner spiked with capsicum (pepper).

You could also top these cakes with maple syrup or jam, leaving out the onion and cilantro if you wish.

TESTING ARTICHOKES FOR DONENESS

To test artichokes for doneness, pull up on a leaf after the artichokes have steamed 30 minutes or so. If the artichoke is thoroughly cooked, the leaf will pull out easily. If it refuses to yield, steam another 10 minutes or so.

Vegetable Corn Cakes

▼

FEEDS 4 IN 30 MINUTES
8–10 3-INCH PANCAKES
About 50¢ each

¾ cup unbleached all-purpose flour
2 ½ teaspoons baking powder
1 tablespoon granulated sugar
1 cup yellow cornmeal
¾ teaspoon salt
1 cup raw vegetable, grated (winter squash,
eggplant, potato)
¼ cup onion, finely chopped
1 large egg
1 cup milk
2 tablespoons vegetable oil
1 cup corn, fresh, frozen or canned
¼ cup cilantro leaves
Salsa
Plain yogurt for garnish

In a medium bowl, stir together the flour, baking powder, sugar, cornmeal, and salt.

In a second medium bowl, mix the vegetable and onion. Add the egg, milk, and oil. Stir to mix.

Stir corn and cilantro into the flour mixture. Pour the vegetable mixture over this and barely mix with a fork.

Preheat griddle or skillet over medium-high heat, coating with oil. For each cake, ladle ½ cup batter onto the hot griddle. Cook on the first side until golden brown and bubbly on top. Turn and cook until done on the second side. Serve two cakes plain or topped with tomato salsa and plain yogurt.

> **A CALORIE-SAVING TIP**
> If you want to save calories as well as money, wipe the hot griddle with wax paper instead of having to grease it. This way, the pancakes won't stick to the pan or to your hips.

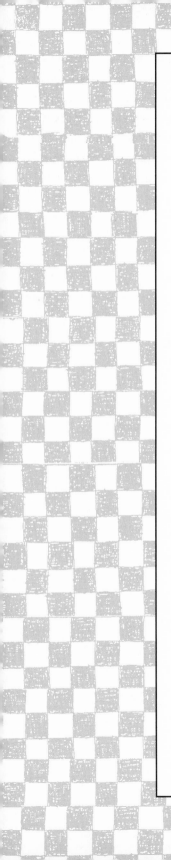

Red Meats

▼

Red meat consumption in this country has taken a dive. For all the reasons you've heard numerous times—cholesterol, cost, we are eating less red meat.

I have noticed a new direction at the supermarket, however. The law of supply and demand seems to be working. Prices for red meat are coming down. Whereas a steak might have been as costly as caviar a couple of years ago, now the price is returning to the realm of possibility.

One belief of mine is that it is risky to latch on to any food trend with too much vigor. As I've said before, the best approach to good nutrition is to eat a broad and varied diet of unprocessed foods—and this includes red meat.

The meats in these recipes are in concert with other things, usually vegetables. The meat servings never exceed three ounces per diner. There are no costly cuts of meat represented here. The recipes in this chapter make use of the less-choice cuts of meat, which are often sold under a vast and confusing array of names. Round steak, for example, can have no less than a dozen different names, and with prices that vary as much as $2.00 a pound.

Red meat, eaten once a week, is special. Prepared simply, with fresh vegetables and careful seasoning, it makes a meal that you will look forward to.

Beef Cilantro Stir-Fry

▼

FEEDS 4 IN 30 MINUTES
About $1.00 per serving

1 pound beef round
¼ cup reduced-sodium soy sauce
½ teaspoon sugar
½ teaspoon rice vinegar
3 or 4 drops hot oil or Tabasco sauce
2 cups rice, uncooked
3 tablespoons cooking oil
2 cucumbers, cut into julienne strips (and peeled if skin is bitter)
¼ cup sesame seeds
1 cup fresh cilantro, packed

Half-freeze (or only half-thaw) beef to facilitate cutting. With the sharpest knife you own, trim fat and then cut across the grain—at an angle—into very thin strips. Now cut the strips into 2-inch lengths.

Combine soy sauce, sugar, vinegar, and hot oil. At room temperature, marinate the strips in sauce for at least 30 minutes covered, turning from time to time so all pieces get their turn on the bottom.

Wash cilantro carefully and strip out a full cup of leaves, discarding stems and roots. Meanwhile, cook rice according to package directions. About 5 minutes before serving time, heat 1 tablespoon oil in a 10- or 12-inch skillet or wok until it begins to thin and run to the edges.

Drain meat strips (reserve the marinade). Cook strips in the hot oil, a few at a time. Turn once. Never cook a strip for more than 20–30 seconds. Remove to a reserving dish. Pour all pan juices over the meat and set aside.

In the same skillet, heat the remaining 2 tablespoons of oil until very hot, then add the cucumbers. Stir and turn for 2 minutes, then add sesame seeds. Cook and stir until seeds begin to brown and cucumber looks fried. Now pour reserved marinade into the skillet, add meat and juice, and toss for just 10 seconds. Turn off heat, add cilantro, toss to mix. Serve immediately with rice.

Fajitas

▼

FEEDS 4 IN 1 HOUR 30 MINUTES
(INCLUDES MARINATING TIME)
About 95¢ per serving

One of the hot new trends in Tex Mex cuisine comes from an old favorite of the Texas Mexican. Skirt steaks, known in San Antonio as fajitas, or "little girdles," have long been a standby for one very good reason. Up until very recently, they were cheap. I mean dirt cheap.

The skirt is beef diaphragm muscle, and for many years it was considered by butchers as a sort of throwaway; but the flavor of the skirt far surpasses that of the beef tenderloin and has suddenly become fashionable.

Fajitas are traditionally cooked outside over a charcoal fire, but Merle Ellis has discovered that you can use a heavy, dry cast-iron skillet over high heat with good results—even though it is guaranteed to set off the smoke alarm. (continued)

1¼–1½ pounds skirt steak
½ can of beer
½ cup cooking oil
1 onion, sliced thin

Marinade:
Juice of 1 lime
1 dried red pepper, crushed
1 clove garlic, pressed
Fresh-ground pepper to taste

For assembly:
8 flour tortillas
Sour cream for garnish
Guacamole for garnish
Salsa for garnish

Combine all marinade ingredients and soak the steak covered in the refrigerator about 1 hour. Meanwhile, make a charcoal fire outside (or use the cast-iron skillet method).

Slice meat into about 6-inch pieces and grill quickly, turning once, no more than 3–4 minutes to the side. Cut on the diagonal into thin strips and fold into a warm flour tortilla with sour cream, guacamole, and salsa.

Mexican Beef Flautas
▼
FEEDS 4 IN 1 HOUR
About $1.00 per serving

In Mexico, women work on the street making flautas over braziers of charcoal. These little "flutes" are so delicate and so deftly made they seem a cinch. Containing only about a table spoon or so of highly seasoned filling, the flutes are rolled tightly and look so inviting they are hard to resist. When you get home and try to make them, you gain respect for those women who seem to roll them so effortlessly. It's hard to do.

There are two or three elements that are a must for a golden brown flauta. First, you must heat the corn tortilla over dry heat until it is soft and pliable enough to roll tightly without cracking. This takes about 15 seconds, and the tortilla must be turned once. Second, you must fry the filled flute in a top-quality cooking oil that won't burn over high heat. Getting the flauta in and out within a couple of minutes, turning it only once, takes a little practice. If it's any consolation, even clumsily made flautas taste good, and you will get better at it with practice.

The first recipe—Mexican Beef Flautas—makes use of a cheap cut of beef, say a round steak, skirt, brisket, or chuck, which is boiled and shredded with the grain, the way the Mexicans do. The second recipe—Avocado Flautas—is a vegetarian flauta, made with a dead-ripe avocado. For a presentation that is both dramatic and surprising, serve your guests some of each kind. If you have a cup of leftover pot roast and one avocado that is almost beyond the pale, you can skip the meat-boiling step and proceed. Make recipes of each filling, and you'll have dinner in a snap.

About ½ pound beef (round skirt, brisket, chuck)
½ small onion, chopped fine
2 tablespoons olive oil or other vegetable oil
(continued)

2 tomatoes, 1 sliced thin and 1 chopped
7 ounces tomato sauce
1 jalapeño pepper, chopped, or some red pepper
    flakes
Salt and pepper to taste
Cooking oil
12 corn tortillas

Place beef in a small dry saucepan or skillet. Brown over high heat, searing each side. Barely cover with water, and simmer covered until tender (about 30 minutes).

Meanwhile, in a medium skillet, heat olive oil on medium high and sauté onions until they begin to brown. Add tomato and tomato sauce, jalapeño pepper, and salt and pepper; simmer uncovered while meat is cooking. When meat is tender, shred it using your sharpest knife, and add to the sauce. Simmer uncovered for 10 minutes.

Get everything ready to assemble and cook the flautas. Lay out a plate covered with paper towels to drain the cooked flautas. Use a spatula and fork to turn the flautas easily. Heat about ¾ inch top-quality vegetable oil in a 10-inch skillet over medium-high heat.

Separate the tortillas and soften them by heating (about 15 seconds, turning once) on a hot dry griddle or in a 7-inch skillet. You can also soften them by microwaving for 30 seconds covered.

Assemble the flautas by placing about a tablespoon of sauce in each tortilla and rolling as tightly as possible. Place in the hot oil, flap side down, and fry until golden brown, turning once (2–3 minutes). You can fry about 3 at a time in a 10-inch skillet. Any more than this will cool the oil too much and result in greasy flautas.

Serve the flautas as finger food or on a plate with shredded iceberg lettuce, tomatoes, sour cream, guacamole, and salsa.

> **SELECTING QUALITY OIL**
> High-quality oils can be heated to higher temperatures than other oils without burning, so select an oil appropriate for the job. Canola, olive, and peanut work best.

Avocado Flautas
▼
FEEDS 4 IN 20 MINUTES
About 60¢ per serving

I sometimes serve leftover turkey with a tomatillo sauce in flautas.

2 dead-ripe avocados
½ small onion, chopped fine
Salt to taste
Juice of 1 lemon
1 clove garlic, pressed
Cooking oil
12 corn tortillas
Sour cream for garnish (optional)
Tomatoes, chopped, or salsa for garnish (optional)
Longhorn cheese, grated (optional)

Peel and seed avocados. Mash to a coarse puree with a fork and add salt, lemon juice and garlic. Using this filling, assemble and cook flautas as directed in preceding recipe. Pass garnishes at the table.

Beef Raisin Tacos

▼

FEEDS 4 IN 30 MINUTES
About 85¢ per serving

Filling:
2 tablespoons vegetable oil
1 small onion, chopped
1 pound lean ground beef
1 cup raisins
½ teaspoon cumin
½ teaspoon oregano
Pinch of sugar
1 jalapeño pepper, chopped
1 clove garlic, minced
1 6-ounce can tomato paste
2 cups water
Salt and pepper to taste
12 taco shells
Lettuce for garnish, shredded
Tomato for garnish, chopped
Cheddar cheese for garnish, grated

In a 10-inch skillet, heat oil on medium-high and sauté onion until translucent. Add ground beef and brown over medium heat. Once browned, drain excess oil, add raisins, cumin, oregano, sugar, jalapeño, garlic, tomato paste, and water. Simmer uncovered 15 minutes or until the mixture has a catsuplike consistency. Adjust seasonings with salt and pepper. Serve on heated taco shells or quick-fried corn tortillas, heated in a dry skillet for about 15 seconds each. Top with lettuce, tomato, and cheese.

Joe's Special

▼

FEEDS 4 IN 30 MINUTES
About 90¢ per serving

This is a traditional San Francisco recipe that originated in a restaurant called Joe's. The regulars have grown accustomed to the peculiar way it looks. It is one of those dishes that looks bad but tastes good. It's also very cheap and very easy.

2 tablespoons cooking oil
1 onion, chopped
1 clove garlic, minced
1 pound lean ground beef
1 bunch fresh spinach or 1 10-ounce package
 frozen spinach
4 eggs, slightly beaten
Salt and pepper to taste

In a 10-inch skillet, heat oil on medium-high and sauté onion and garlic in oil until translucent. Add ground beef and brown. Meanwhile, steam spinach, drain well, and chop. (If you're using frozen spinach, just thaw it.) When the meat has browned, drain excess fat. Turn heat to lowest setting. Add spinach, eggs, and salt and pepper. Toss mixture gently with two forks until egg is cooked. Serve immediately. All you need with this meal is a slice of good bread and a piece of fruit.

Curried Meatballs

▼

Meatballs don't have to mean spaghetti. All cultures have their ground-meat dishes, and the peasant cuisines make good use of spices in addition to the meat. The cuisine of India uses an interesting blend of spices for ground-meat dishes that can provide relief from the typical ground meat and tomato sauce routine. This curry is subtle and delicate. If you prefer a bolder curry, increase spices, tasting and adjusting with each addition.

The price per serving counts on using homemade bread crumbs and pre-frozen chicken stock. Resorting to ready-made bread crumbs or canned chicken broth will drive the price per serving up. The bread crumbs can be made from 2 stale English muffins or 2–3 heels of leftover bread crumbled into the mixture.

If you want to make the meatballs quickly, toss the ingredients in the order listed into the food processor. This will produce a marvelous smooth mixture. Or you can simply toss all the ingredients together and mix by hand.

Meatballs:
2 medium onions, chopped fine
1 cup fresh bread crumbs
2 hot green chiles or jalapeño peppers, seeded and chopped fine
Black pepper to taste
⅛ teaspoon ground cinnamon
⅛ teaspoon ground cloves
1 egg, beaten
1½ pounds lean ground lamb or beef
Cooking oil

Sauce:
2 tablespoons butter or margarine
2 tablespoons flour
2 teaspoons curry powder
1½ cups chicken stock, bouillon, or water
⅓ cup evaporated milk or cream
1–1½ cups rice, uncooked

Mix all meatball ingredients together. Barely cover the bottom of a 10-inch skillet with oil and heat over medium-high. Drop meat mixture by the tablespoonful into the hot skillet. Brown meatballs on all sides, a panful at a time, shaking the pan to turn them.

Make a golden roux of butter, flour, and curry powder, then slowly stir in chicken stock and cook about 5 minutes. Add milk and heat to boiling.

When the meatballs are browned, remove all fat from the skillet with a bulb baster. Pour sauce over them, cover, and simmer for 10 minutes.

Cook rice according to package directions and serve curried meatballs over it.

Sliced bell pepper and tomato are the natural complements to this quick and easy curry. Other condiments might include cucumbers in yogurt, chopped peanuts, raisins, coconut, riced hard-cooked eggs, and chutney. Did you notice there's no salt? Good sound spicing cuts down on the need for salt.

Cal-Mex Lasagna

▼

FEEDS 4 IN 1 HOUR 15 MINUTES
About 75¢ per serving

Here is a literal melting pot.

Meat Sauce:
2 tablespoons cooking oil
1 onion, chopped fine
1 clove garlic, pressed
¾ pound lean ground beef
3 medium tomatoes or 2 cups stewed tomatoes, chopped coarse
1 cup chicken stock
1 small (7 ounces) can tomato sauce
Salt and pepper to taste
¼ teaspoon ground cinnamon
¼ cup raisins (or prunes, dates, grapes)

1 8-ounce carton small-curd cottage cheese or ricotta
1 egg
¼ pound jack cheese, shredded
4 corn tortillas
1 7-ounce can green chiles or 6 Anaheim or Poblano chiles, seeded and deveined

Preheat oven to 350° F. In a 10-inch skillet, heat oil to medium-high and sauté onion and garlic until translucent. Add ground beef and cook until all pink color has disappeared. Drain excess grease. Now add remaining sauce ingredients and simmer uncovered for 20–30 minutes or until thickened to a catsuplike consistency.

Meanwhile, combine cottage cheese with egg in a small bowl. Place shredded cheese onto a piece of waxed paper. Grease a casserole dish 10x6x1¾ inches.

Heat tortillas in a hot, dry skillet about 15 seconds to the side. Place two tortillas on the bottom of casserole dish. Cover with half the green chiles, half the cottage cheese mixture, then half the meat sauce. Cover with the other two tortillas and the rest of the green chiles, cottage cheese, and meat sauce. Top with the shredded cheese.

Bake until bubbly and cheese is beginning to brown (about 25 minutes). Allow to cool 10 minutes before cutting into squares. Delicious with a simple green salad.

Zesty Lamb Sauté

▼

FEEDS 4 IN 30 MINUTES
About $1.00 per serving

Take care when buying lamb that you are get-ting the best deal. This week, I found shoulder chops for $2.25 a pound. Next to that was lamb stew meat for $5.25. Three dollars a pound for cutting up the meat? Outrageous. You can also use this recipe with leftover lamb, in which case you can halve the preparation time.

1 tablespoon olive oil
1–1½ pounds lean lamb chunks
2 medium onions, chopped coarse
5 cloves garlic, sliced thin
½ teaspoon paprika
¼ teaspoon black pepper
Juice of 1 lemon
Salt to taste
¼ cup fresh parsley, chopped

In a 10-inch skillet, heat oil on medium-high and sauté lamb chunks until brown on all sides. Remove meat from skillet and set aside. In the same juices sauté the onions and garlic until golden. Turn heat to medium low. Stir in paprika, pepper, and lemon juice. Return lamb chunks to skillet. Salt, cover, and cook until lamb is tender (about 20 minutes). Just before serving, toss parsley with lamb. Good with egg noodles.

Fruited Lamb Balls

▼

FEEDS 4 IN 1 HOUR
About 80¢ per serving

1 pound lean ground lamb
1 tablespoon olive oil
1 large onion, chopped coarse
4 cloves garlic, pressed
1 cup chicken broth
1 cup dry white wine
1-inch piece stick cinnamon
2 teaspoons coriander seed
½ teaspoon ground ginger or thumb-sized piece
    of fresh ginger, grated
¼ teaspoon black pepper
12 prunes, pitted
¼ cup raisins
2 teaspoons honey
1 teaspoon sesame seeds

Form lamb into 8 equal-sized balls. In a 10-inch skillet brown on all sides in oil over medi-um heat. Add onion and garlic. Cook until onion begins to brown. Meanwhile, add broth, wine, cinnamon, coriander, and ginger to meat. Add prunes and raisins. Cover and sim-mer until meat cooks and fruits plump (20–30 minutes). Remove lid, raise heat, and cook sauce until thick. Then stir in honey, sprinkle with sesame seeds, and serve. Good with bul-gur or brown rice.

Kat's Lamb Moussaka

▼

FEEDS 5 IN 1 HOUR 30 MINUTES
About 75¢ per serving

The less expensive shoulder cut of lamb works well in this braised skillet dish. If you get fairly large but thin-sliced chops, you can make four chops serve six people. This moussaka is shockingly easy to do, makes very little mess in the kitchen, and is cheap. This dish clearly shows how sometimes the simplest ingredients, prepared with a sophisticated technique, can produce a meal to please the most particular diner.

4 large, thin-cut lamb shoulder chops
3 onions, chopped coarse
4 garlic cloves, chopped coarse
1 28-ounce can tomatoes
1 teaspoon cinnamon
Salt and pepper to taste

In a dry 10-inch skillet, brown the chops, onions, and garlic over medium-high heat. Constantly stir onions and garlic in and around the chops. When the onions begin to caramelize (the secret to the way this dish tastes), add a couple of tablespoons of water to prevent sticking, cover, and steam 1–2 minutes. This entire browning process takes at least 10 minutes and requires fairly constant attention.

Now add tomatoes and juice, cinnamon, and salt and pepper; reduce heat and simmer uncovered for about 1 hour. Just before serving, pull meat into large chunks and discard bone. Serve with rice, a green salad with lots of garlic in the vinaigrette, a loaf of French bread, and a robust burgundy. With apples and cheese for dessert, this dish makes wonderful company fare.

California Pork and Beans

▼

FEEDS 4 IN 40 MINUTES
About $1.00 per serving

They'll never believe you in Boston, but here it is. California Szechuan. Try this when fresh beans are at the peak of the harvest—both cheap and flavorful. Snoop around for the pork and get the best buy. Chops, cutlets, or a piece of a roast make good choices. Buy 3–4 ounces of lean meat per diner.

If you haven't stir-fried before, you may not be as fast as the cook in a Chinese restaurant, but once you learn to organize the work in its logical steps, you can prepare this and most stir-fried dishes in the time it takes to cook a pot of rice.

Batter:
½ teaspoon salt
1 egg white
1 tablespoon sherry
2 teaspoons cornstarch

Beans:

1 pound fresh pork, sliced into strips (½ inch thick and 1–2 inches long)
1 pound fresh green beans, washed and snapped
3 green onions, chopped fine
4 whole dried hot chile peppers
2 cloves garlic, chopped fine
2 tablespoons minced fresh ginger or 1 teaspoon powdered ginger

Sauce:

¼ cup reduced-sodium soy sauce
4 tablespoons sherry
1 teaspoon sugar
1 tablespoon cornstarch
¼ cup chicken broth or water
1 teaspoon sesame oil

4 tablespoons peanut oil or other cooking oil

Mix salt, egg white, sherry and cornstarch for batter and whip together with a fork until frothy. Add meat strips to batter. Using your hands, rub batter into meat. Allow to stand about 15 minutes.

In a small bowl, combine ginger, green onions, garlic, and chile peppers and set aside.

In another small bowl, mix together sauce ingredients; stir until smooth.

In a 10-inch skillet or a wok, heat 1 tablespoon peanut oil at the highest setting until a haze forms and the oil begins to thin. Add beans, standing back to avoid being splattered. Stir and fry beans until they are cooked but crunchy (about 3 minutes; the skins just begin to blister and brown when done). Use a slotted spoon to remove to a bowl.

Allow oil to regain full heat. Add 1 tablespoon or more if pan looks dry. When oil is smoking hot again, carefully add meat strips, a few at a time and 1 layer deep. Cook on each side until crust forms (about 30 seconds). Push to the side of pan and add more strips to cook. When all the meat has been cooked (no more than 3–4 minutes), remove with slotted spoon to the bowl of beans.

Allow oil to regain full heat, again adding 1–2 more to make 3 tablespoons. Add the onion, pepper, ginger, and garlic mixture and stir-fry for 10 seconds. Replace beans and meat; stir to mix thoroughly. Pour sauce over and stir-fry briskly for 1 minute. Serve immediately along with rice or cooked noodles. You can remove the whole peppers before taking the dish to the table if there are any cowards waiting.

Enchiladas Aztecas

▼

FEEDS 4 IN 45 MINUTES
About $1.00 per serving

1½ pounds pork shoulder
1 onion, chopped
2 ribs celery, cut on the diagonal
½ cup chili sauce or catsup
½ ounce unsweetened chocolate
1 8-ounce can tomato sauce
Tabasco sauce to taste
Salt and pepper to taste
8 corn tortillas
1 cup sour cream or yogurt
(continued)

Trim bone and fat from pork. Cut meat into about ½-inch cubes. Render fat from trimmings, then brown cubes of meat in fat over high heat. Remove trimmings and discard. Lower heat to medium and add chopped onion and half of the celery. Sauté until onion is translucent. Add chili sauce, chocolate, and ⅔ of the tomato sauce. Heat, stirring until chocolate melts. Add Tabasco and salt and pepper. Lower heat. Simmer for 15 minutes. Heat tortillas in a dry skillet (15 seconds per side), then remove to a 6x10x¾-inch baking dish.

Preheat oven to 400° F. Spoon heaping teaspoonfuls of meat mixture into tortillas, roll, and place flap side down in a neat row in the baking dish. After all tortillas are filled, spoon any remaining filling onto and around rolls. Spoon a strip of sour cream or yogurt down the center of the rolls. Now make a ribbon of remaining tomato sauce on top of sour cream. Sprinkle with remaining celery. Heat uncovered in the oven for 10 minutes or until hot.

Greek Pork

▼

FEEDS 6 IN 1 HOUR
About $1.00 per serving

If you don't have access to Greek olives, just substitute green olives in this recipe; broken ones will do fine. For the pork, you should see what you can get that will produce the most lean meat for the least money, such as shoulder chops or a small rolled roast. The prices of these things vary. What you are after is about a pound and a half of fairly lean chunks. The friend who gave me this recipe actually prefers the recipe made with chicken. If pork is out of the question, use a 3-pound fryer cut into serving pieces.

1½ pounds lean pork chunks
1 tablespoon olive oil
1 clove garlic, chopped
2 tablespoons slivered almonds
1 onion, peeled and sliced
½ pound fresh mushrooms, sliced
Salt and pepper to taste
1 cup dry white wine
1 teaspoon fresh mint, chopped, or ½ teaspoon dried
2 tablespoons fresh parsley, minced
12 Greek olives, pitted

Heat oil in a 10-inch skillet over medium-high heat, and brown meat chunks, garlic, and almonds. When the meat is browning nicely, add onions and mushrooms. Sauté until onion turns translucent. Add remaining ingredients, except olives. Cover and simmer until meat is tender (about 30 minutes). About 5 minutes before serving time, add olives and heat through. Good over rice or bulgur.

Tamale Pie

▼

FEEDS 8 IN 45 MINUTES
About 90¢ per serving

Tamale pie is almost as American as apple. At least to those of us who grew up in the Southwest, this suppertime standby was as common as Kraft dinners.

Substitute freely between bell pepper and celery, using what you have on hand to make ½ cup total. Use canned refritos (refried beans) if you must, but you'll save the most money and get the best taste if you use cooked and refried dried pinto beans. The salsa can be fresh or canned. For cheese, use cheddar or a mix of cheeses you have on hand. Although we prefer homemade corn bread batter—cheaper and tastier—you can plug in a 15-ounce box of corn bread mix. It will have too much sugar, and that would make any Tex-Mex cowboy scream caramba, but it is fast.

2 cups refried beans
1 pound lean ground beef
½ cup onion, chopped
½ cup bell pepper or celery, chopped
½ cup chunky salsa, mild or hot
½ cup ripe olives, sliced
Salt and pepper to taste

Topping:
Corn bread topping, see next recipe
¾ cup cheddar cheese or mixture, grated

Make refritos by first cooking 1 cup of dried pintos in boiling salted water to cover until tender, about 2 hours. Then drain and mash the beans in an oiled skillet over medium heat until cooked and dry.

Preheat the oven to 350° F. Sauté beef with onion, green pepper or celery in a 10-inch skillet over medium-high heat, stirring until meat is cooked and vegetables are translucent. Drain any excess fat. Stir in salsa, olives, and salt and pepper.

Coat a 9-inch deep-dish pie pan with cooking spray. Cover the bottom and sides of the pan with refried beans. Then pour meat mixture over that. Top with corn bread batter. Sprinkle with cheese, then bake 30–35 minutes, until crust is lightly browned.

Allow the pie to rest 10 minutes on a rack before cutting into pie slices. Serve garnished with shredded iceberg lettuce and chopped tomatoes, if desired.

Corn Bread Topping

▼

FEEDS 8 IN 15 MINUTES
About 20¢ per serving

Dress up this corn bread topping by crumbling a piece of bacon into the batter, adding a couple of tablespoons of chopped onion and/or bell pepper, or a tablespoon of chili powder. If you like your food picante, chop in a fresh jalapeño. If you wish to bake this as plain country corn bread, preheat the oven to 400° F. Heat the bacon grease in a black cast-iron 10-inch skillet and pour the batter into the skillet and bake in the oven about 10–12 minutes. The top will be dull. Place it under the broiler to brown, then serve immediately with plenty of sweet butter and syrup.

3 tablespoons bacon grease or vegetable oil
1 cup yellow cornmeal
½ cup unbleached all-purpose flour
½ teaspoon salt
½ teaspoon soda
½ teaspoon baking powder
1 tablespoon sugar
1 cup buttermilk
1 large egg

Heat grease in a 10-inch cast-iron skillet until smoking hot. Meanwhile, mix dry ingredients in a medium bowl. Stir in buttermilk and egg, mixing thoroughly. Pour in hot bacon grease and stir.

Spread this corn bread batter over the meat mixture and bake.

Dutch-Oven Dinner

▼

FEEDS 6 IN 1 HOUR 30 MINUTES
About 80¢ per serving

A midwinter dinner made in a cast-iron Dutch oven. Children love the mixture of meat loaf and root vegetables braised together.

Meat loaf:
1½ pounds lean ground beef
2 slices of bread
½ cup water
1 egg white
Salt and pepper to taste

¼ cup minced onion
1 teaspoon Worcestershire sauce
½ teaspoon Dijon mustard

Vegetables:
1⅔ cup beef stock
4 cups scraped raw vegetables:
   Potatoes, Rutabagas, Carrots, Onions,
   Turnips, Celery

In a large mixing bowl crumble the ground beef. Tear bread into small pieces in the bowl, then add remaining meat loaf ingredients. Mix together with your hands.

Form a loaf shape and refrigerate a few minutes. Meanwhile, prepare the vegetables, then preheat a dry Dutch oven and brown the meat loaf on all sides over medium-high heat.

Once the meat loaf is browned all over, lift it out of the pan. Cover the bottom of the pan with the raw vegetables. Place the meat loaf back on top of the vegetables, pour the stock over, cover, and turn the heat down to a simmer. Cook about 1 hour, or until the dinner is done.

To serve, lift the meat and vegetables onto a warm platter and slice the meat.

**MAKING GRAVY
FROM PAN DRIPPINGS**
Make a gravy from the good pan drippings, by dissolving 2 tablespoons of flour into ½ cup water, then pour it into the drippings. Bring slowly to a boil, stirring. Taste and adjust the seasonings. Serve gravy with meat loaf and vegetables.

Not-So-Sloppy Joes

▼

FEEDS 4 IN 45 MINUTES
About 90¢ per serving

Serve these family favorites open-faced on hamburger buns with plenty of shredded iceberg lettuce on top. It's dinner in 45 minutes and with only one pan to wash.

1 pound lean ground beef
2 medium onions, finely chopped
1 bell pepper (any color), seeded and finely chopped
8 large garlic cloves, finely chopped
2 tablespoons chili powder
1 28-ounce can Italian plum tomatoes, drained and chopped, juice reserved
½ cup catsup
2 teaspoons red wine vinegar
2 teaspoons Worcestershire sauce
3 tablespoons fresh parsley, chopped
Salt and pepper to taste

Brown beef in a cast-iron Dutch oven over medium-high heat until it begins to lose its pink color, about 5 minutes.

Reduce the heat to medium, and add onions, pepper, and garlic one item at a time as you chop them. Take your time; let this mixture cook down about 15 minutes. Mix in the chili powder and continue cooking 2 minutes. Add tomatoes, catsup, vinegar, and Worcestershire. Cook until the vegetables are tender and the mixture is thick. Stir frequently. If the mixture seems too thick and threatens to stick to the bottom, add a little reserved tomato juice. Season with salt and pepper, then spoon onto hot hamburger buns. Top with generous handfuls of shredded iceberg lettuce and serve open faced. A kosher pickle and a few crunchy vegetables or chips completes this dinner.

Stir-fried Skillet Supper

▼

FEEDS 4 IN 15 MINUTES
About 80¢ per serving

Boil a pot of noodles, stir fry beef with green onions and mushrooms and you've got a healthy, cheap meal quick.

4 packages of Ramen noodles
1 tablespoon sesame oil
2 cloves garlic, coarsely chopped
1 bunch green onions, sliced on the diagonal
1 cup mushrooms, sliced thin
1 pound lean ground beef
2 tablespoons rice vinegar
2 tablespoons barbecue sauce
Salt and pepper to taste

Cook noodles in a large pan of lightly salted boiling water just until limp, 3 minutes. Do not add the flavoring packet. Drain and reserve.

Meanwhile, in a wok or 10-inch skillet over high heat, cook the garlic, green onions, and mushrooms a minute or so in the sesame oil. Then add the ground beef and stir fry just until the meat loses its pink cast. Add rice vinegar and cook 30 seconds more.

Stir in the barbecue sauce and salt and pepper. Serve the stir fry over Ramen noodles.

Homemade Hamburger's Assistant

▼

MAKES 1½ OUNCES IN 5 MINUTES,
SEASONS 7 POUNDS MEAT
About 10¢ per serving

Believe me. You can help hamburger without letting some manufacturer do your thinking for you. Make your own hamburger's assistant. Then brown the meat with an onion. Cook a pot of noodles, rice, or spaghetti—depending on what you have on hand, and you've not only helped the hamburger, you've helped the grocery budget and the family's health.

However, this homemade hamburger helper wouldn't be any bargain if you looked over the long list of spices and herbs then took off for the local supermarket to buy those products in lovely little glass jars. The way to beat that system is to shop your local food co-op where the herbs and spices are sold in bulk. A couple of scoops of each herb is less than $2.00, and you'll have plenty left over to restock your basic pantry. Store the herbs in baby food jars, labeled, and you'll save yourself a bundle.

1 tablespoon basil
2 tablespoons oregano
¼ cup parsley flakes
1 teaspoon fennel seed
1 teaspoon savory
1 teaspoon marjoram

½ teaspoon red pepper flakes
1 tablespoon black pepper
1 tablespoon salt
1 teaspoon sugar
1 teaspoon garlic salt

Combine these spices in a clean airtight jar and store in the pantry.

Hamburger Stir-Fry

▼

FEEDS 4 IN 20 MINUTES
About $1.00 per serving

1 pound lean ground beef
1 medium onion, chopped
1 tablespoon homemade hamburger's assistant
*   spice mix (or to taste)*
16 ounces tomatoes and juice
12 ounces spaghetti or noodles
Parmesan cheese to garnish, grated

In a 10-inch skillet or wok over medium-high heat, brown the hamburger meat along with onion and spice mix. Add tomatoes and juice, turn heat to low, and simmer about 10 minutes, adjusting seasonings to taste.

Meanwhile, cook spaghetti to al dente according to package directions. Drain.

To serve, arrange pasta on a large serving platter and top with sauce. Dust the top with grated Parmesan cheese.

Bundt Loaf

▼

FEEDS 12–16 IN 1 HOUR 30 MINUTES
About 75¢ per serving

Serve with mashed potatoes, peas and carrots and plain tossed salad.

½ cup honey
1 cup milk
2 large eggs
6 slices white bread
3 pounds lean ground beef or turkey
2 pounds ground pork
Salt and pepper to taste
2 large yellow onions, finely chopped
½ cup catsup or barbecue sauce
2 tablespoons prepared mustard

Preheat the oven to 375° F. Thoroughly grease a 12-inch round bundt pan and set aside.

In a large mixing bowl whisk together the honey, milk, and eggs. Tear the bread into this mixture and let it soak up the moisture. Crumble the ground meats into this mixture. Season with salt and pepper. Add onions and mix thoroughly with your hands.

Turn the mixture into the bundt pan, pressing down thoroughly, to pack it in tight. Bake 1 hour and 15 minutes. Remove from the oven and turn the meat loaf out onto a cookie sheet with sides.

Mix the catsup and mustard together and smear it over the meat loaf. Return it to the oven and bake an additional 15 minutes. Let the meat loaf stand a few minutes before cutting it.

Daddy's Meat Loaf

▼

FEEDS 6 IN 1 HOUR 30 MINUTES
About 90¢ per serving

½ cup milk
1 egg
¾ cup rolled oats
1 pound lean ground beef or turkey
½ pound ground pork
3 tablespoons Worcestershire sauce
1 small tomato, diced
½ cup EACH diced celery, onion, green pepper
2 large cloves garlic, finely chopped
1 teaspoon EACH dried basil, thyme, oregano
Salt and pepper to taste
4 thick slices bacon
½ cup catsup

Preheat the oven to 425° F. In a large mixing bowl whisk the milk and eggs together then stir in the oats. Crumble in the ground meats and mix thoroughly.

Add the Worcestershire, tomatoes, celery, onion, green pepper, garlic, basil, thyme, oregano, salt and pepper. Mix thoroughly with your hands.

Press it into a standard loaf pan baking dish. Lay the bacon strips on the top and drizzle the catsup over the top. Bake 60 minutes, or until done.

WHERE'S THE BEEF?

Not so long ago, hamburger was hamburger. And it was usually less than a dollar a pound. But then we began to worry about fats and cholesterol and before you knew it we had a dizzying array of choices under the heading "ground beef."

Read the fine print on labels today, and you're likely to see fat contents ranging from 30 percent down to a mere 4 percent, with prices that range all over the map.

So what's the best buy? Today, I bought a pound each of several different ground beef products. At home, I weighed them into equal 4-ounce patties, peppered them, then broiled them on a rack about 4 minutes to the side.

I was trying to see how much fat and moisture dripped out, what each hamburger weighed when it was cooked, how it tasted, and how much it cost—per bite. There was almost no difference in taste or moisture-fat loss between the 22-percent and 16-percent fat hamburgers.

Drop the fat content to 10 or 4 percent and the hamburger got a little dicey. Dense, gray, and solid as a pat of wet cement, this lowest fat product seemed to need the most seasoning, and it certainly cost the most.

"Healthy Choice" is a Con-Agra reconstituted ground beef product that contains a solution of beef stock, "Oatrim"™, water and encapsulated salt. The raw produce contains only 4 percent fat, yet derives 28 percent of its calories from fat. As far as we're concerned, it's too processed and too pricey.

That poor 30-percent fat burger shrank by nearly half and didn't seem to be a bargain in either the health department or at the bank.

For our money, we're sticking to mid-range ground beef products. We like the taste. They don't cost too much. And we can—to use an old fashioned/newly stylish term—stretch these with ground beef dishes with various complex carbohydrates for interesting new tastes.

COMPARISONS OF GROUND BEEF PRODUCTS

4-ounce patty raw makes a cooked weight of:

	Fat	$/Pound	Ounces
"Healthy Choice" Extra Lean Ground Beef	4%	$2.99	3.2
Leanest Ground Beef	10%	2.28	3.1
Extra Lean Ground Beef	16%	1.98	3.0
Lean Ground Beef	22%	1.78	2.9
Regular Ground Beef	30%	1.19	2.3

Santa Fe Stove Top

▼

FEEDS 6 IN 35 MINUTES
about 80¢ per serving

We hardly ever say the C word around here anymore. I mean, just whisper the word casserole and people run for the exits.

But casseroles have served a useful function in the kitchen for a long time. The one-dish dinner is always attractive to the cook because it means fewer dishes to wash. And what used to be called "meat stretchers," we now know are probably life stretchers as well, because they load a casserole with complex carbohydrates and knock back the saturated fats found in traditional meat-laden casseroles.

This latest concoction appeals to me for summer cooking for another good reason as well. It's cooked on the top of the stove, then placed under the broiler to brown. This keeps the kitchen cool since you only fire up the oven for 5 minutes or so. It is also a fuel efficient way to cook the meal.

I use a gorgeous porcelain-clad cast-iron casserole dish that goes from stove top or oven to table and can be placed in the freezer as well. I found this wonder at the Goodwill. You know, like Le Creuset, only instead of the $75.00 price tag I'd have to fork over for one of these beauties at a gourmet shop, I got mine for a couple of bucks at the thrift store. It pays to wander through these places frequently.

You could also use pyroceram cookware to prepare this casserole. If you wish, you can cook the casserole, divide it in half, and freeze the last half for later use. Thaw, reheat and brown the top before serving. All you need to accompany is a torn leaf lettuce salad, some flour tortillas, and a bottle of micro-brewed local beer, icy cold.

¾ *pound lean ground beef*
4 cloves garlic, peeled and pressed
1 medium onion, peeled and finely chopped
1 medium bell pepper (any color), seeded and
  finely chopped
Salt and pepper to taste
1 tablespoon chili powder
1 cup corn (fresh, frozen, or canned)
1 14½-ounce can stewed tomatoes
½ cup long grain rice, uncooked
1 cup water
1 cup broken tortilla chips
1 cup cheddar cheese, shredded

In a fireproof 3-quart casserole dish, brown the ground beef over medium heat with garlic, onion, bell pepper, salt and pepper, and chili powder about 10 minutes.

Stir in corn, tomatoes, rice and water. Cover. Reduce heat and simmer the mixture undisturbed for 20 minutes.

Preheat the broiler during the last 5 minutes of cooking time. Remove the lid from the casserole, sprinkle with broken tortilla chips and shredded cheddar. Broil about 3 minutes until bubbly and brown.

Inside-Out Hamburger Pie

▼

FEEDS 6 IN 1 HOUR
About 85¢ per serving

Crust:
2 heels of bread, processed into fine crumbs
½ cup tomato sauce
1 pound lean ground beef
¼ cup finely chopped onion
⅛ teaspoon dried oregano
Salt and generous grinding of black pepper

Filling:
1½ cup instant uncooked white rice
1 cup water
1½ cups tomato sauce
1 cup cheddar cheese, grated
Salt and pepper to taste

Preheat the oven to 350° F. Combine ½ cup of the bread crumbs with tomato sauce, ground beef, finely chopped onion, oregano, salt, and ground pepper. Mix thoroughly with a wooden spoon, then press into a 9-inch metal pie pan forming a "crust."

Pour into the crust the rice, water, tomato sauce, and half the cheese. Cover with aluminum foil, and bake 25 minutes. Uncover, sprinkle with remaining cheese and bread crumbs, then bake uncovered 15 minutes longer, or until rice is tender.

Let the pie stand 10 minutes or so before cutting into 6 wedges.

Retro Slumgullion

▼

FEEDS 6 IN 30 MINUTES
About 75¢ per serving

Made the old fashioned way, slumgullion is gray, greasy, and not too healthy by today's standards. We fed the first batch to the Muensterlanders.

Second time out, we updated the recipe. We doubled the pasta and halved the meat. We used lean ground beef and pumped up the nutrition and taste with the addition of more onions and peppers. The slumgullion began to seem more acceptable by today's yardstick.

Still, served up on the plate, it looked like a sloppy joe that was more slop than joe. A pale gray blob on the plate, it looked like something from your worst nightmare of college dorm food. Then my husband, Joe, suggested throwing in some frozen peas.

The first time we did this, Joe got up from the table, got the peas out of the freezer, stirred a handful into his own steaming serving and let it stand a few moments to thaw before taking a bite.

Suddenly the slumgullion soared. What a little bright green color and an explosion of sweet taste those peas offered. Plain frozen peas lifted slumgullion right out of the slum.

1 tablespoon canola oil
2 medium onions, peeled and diced
2 medium bell peppers, seeded and diced
2 cups elbow macaroni, uncooked
1 pound lean ground beef

1 14½-ounce can tomatoes and juice plus
    1 can of water
Salt and pepper to taste
2 cups frozen peas

In a large stew pot over medium-high heat, brown in hot oil the onions, bell peppers, and macaroni. Stir until all the ingredients are coated with oil and the vegetables are beginning to brown on the edges.

Crumble the ground beef into the mixture and brown. Add tomatoes and juice, water, and lower the heat to a simmer. Cover and cook about 20 minutes, until the macaroni is firm but cooked al dente. Add water as necessary if it seems to be sticking on the bottom.

When the macaroni is tender, but not falling apart, season to taste with salt and pepper, stir in the frozen peas, cover, and remove from heat for 5 minutes. Serve in soup bowls with plenty of crusty French bread to soak up the good juices.

Beans

▼

One of the kitchen rituals when I was growing up was called "picking the beans." My mother would sit down at night under a strong lamp, and spread a sack full of pinto beans across the kitchen table. Cleaning the beans had been her earliest kitchen responsibility on the ranch where she grew up—along with cleaning the lamps. With infinite care she would pick through the beans, discarding rocks, twigs, and even broken beans. Only perfect beans went into the pot.

She would carefully scoop the perfect beans into an ancient, round-bottomed pot, run cold clear water over them, and leave them to soak. The next morning, she would take out a piece of salt pork, rinse it, cut deep slashes in it, sniff it, and comment on its quality. She was utterly discriminating about salt pork. Then she'd drain the beans from their soaking water, cover them with fresh cold water, bury the salt pork in the middle of the beans, set the pot on the back of the stove, turn it to its lowest setting, and go off to work.

Daddy was an electrician. He was in and out of the house during the day. He kept an eye on the beans: adjusting the fire, adding water as necessary, tasting for seasoning. We all came home for lunch in those days. The first question my mother would ask when she got home was, "How are the beans doing?" My daddy's answer would be thoughtful and detailed.

About sundown, Daddy made the corn bread (see Daddy's Corn Bread, p. 136); then after a full 24 hours of anticipation and preparation, we would sit down to a meal of steaming pinto beans, hot crumbly corn bread, and spinach. It was a feast.

It never occurred to me then that beans were a cheap meal. So much attention and care were given to their preparation, I thought they were the best thing we had every week. When we had them on Sundays—which we frequently did—I thought it perfectly appropriate because they required the most ritual. It never dawned on me that times were hard.

I'm sorry to say that I haven't passed on this sense of mystery and ritual about beans to my own children. I have learned that I can cook beans without soaking them at all. I can give them a quick, cursory glance for rocks and twigs. I can rinse them in a colander in two minutes flat. I can put them in a crockpot and forget them. I think this is what is meant by the saying, "She could never cook it like Mama did." In the service of efficiency, something has been lost.

Now, you may not be interested in making a ritual of beans, but you can feel good about serving them to the family once a week. They will be, hands down, the least expensive meal you can ever achieve. Beans are a good source of vegetable protein and, in combination with whole grains, make a complementary protein meal as nutritious as a T-bone steak. There is great variety in the taste of beans. Using different techniques, you can offer meals that are quite cheap without being boring or repetitious. Brown rice, corn bread, and tortillas are the simple, natural complements to beans.

If you live in the mountains, or wish to save tomorrow's time, soak the beans overnight in water to cover. Before you start, just take a quick look for stray rocks or dirt clods. Discard those, then run water over the beans in a colander, then pour them into a big pot with fresh, cold water to cover by an inch and cook away. Beans will expand up to three times the volume you started with, so choose a pot that's big enough to hold the beans as they cook and swell.

The electric crockpot is an ideal device for cooking beans all day with no attention. As I mentioned before, I never soak beans anymore. But if you live at a high elevation, where water boils at a lower temperature, you will probably need to soak beans and extend the cooking period and add more water to maintain a soupy consistency. The one-hour fast soak is a good solution for cooks who don't think about beans a day ahead. Simply cover beans generously with water, raise to a good rolling boil, put a lid on, turn the fire off, and let stand an hour. Drain and begin cooking in fresh water. But if you live at an elevation as low as 2,000 feet above sea level or less, you won't need to soak beans at all.

Beans are better the second day. Cover and refrigerate overnight. I know you won't be able to resist eating a bowl or two the first day, but believe me they're much improved by a long sleep in the refrigerator overnight. To freeze them, scoop the cold beans and soup into ziplock bags and place, one layer deep, in the freezer for a quick freeze. Then to reheat, just transfer the frozen beans to a microwaveable bowl and heat in the microwave until bubbling at 100% (HIGH) power.

The basic procedures for beans in this chapter produce a kind of bean soup. You will learn the joys of pot liquor if you'll just serve them plain. Sometimes the simplest things are the best, after all.

Black-Eyed Peas

▼

FEEDS 6 IN 1 HOUR (AT HIGH ALTITUDE
MAY TAKE A LITTLE LONGER)
About 20¢ per serving

The primary advantage of dried black-eyed peas over other dried legumes is that they will cook within one hour. The secondary advantage is that they taste so good. Being from the South, I grew up eating black-eyed peas and corn bread. In the summer, some okra was thrown in for good measure. Old-fashioned Southern style, cooked with salt pork and served with spinach, is a wonderful well-balanced meal; it provides complete protein as well as lots of vitamins and minerals, and the cost is scandalously low. The last but not least advantage to black-eyed peas is that if you eat them on New Year's Day, you will have good luck all year long.

1 pound dried, unsoaked black-eyed peas
1½ quarts hot tap water
1 tablespoon olive oil or bacon drippings
1 teaspoon salt

Combine peas with water, oil and salt. Bring to a boil, then reduce heat; cover and simmer until tender (about 1 hour). Don't forget to make a pan of corn bread to go with this.

Hoppin' John

▼

FEEDS 8 IN 1 HOUR
About 40¢ per serving

This recipe is based on another of those traditional combinations from the South that provides complete protein.

6 strips bacon, diced
1 onion, chopped fine
1 pound dried black-eyed peas
1½ quarts hot tap water
1 teaspoon salt
1 cup long-grain rice
Salt and pepper to taste
Tabasco sauce to taste

In the bottom of a large saucepan, fry bacon and onion on medium-high heat until translucent, stirring so that they don't stick. Add dried peas, water, and salt. Raise to a boil, then reduce heat; cover and simmer until peas are tender (about 1 hour). Meanwhile, in a separate pan, cook rice according to package directions. Once the peas and rice are both done, drain and reserve liquid from peas, combine peas with rice, and season with salt and pepper and Tabasco. The reserved liquid is what we call pot liquor and is highly prized by some of us southerners. It tastes best if you drink it straight out of the pot.

Colorful Cranberry Beans

FEEDS 6 IN 2 HOURS 30 MINUTES
About 45¢ per serving

2 cups dried cranberry beans
6 cups salted water
¼ cup olive oil
2 onions, chopped coarse
2 cloves garlic, minced
6 medium tomatoes, peeled or 1 large
    (28 ounces) can tomatoes, chopped
1½ teaspoons basil
1½ teaspoons oregano
Salt and pepper to taste
2 cups winter squash (hard-shelled), peeled,
    seeded, and cut into 1-inch cubes
½ cup corn (fresh, frozen, or canned)

Place beans and water in large pot, bring to a boil, salt the water lightly, then reduce heat and let simmer.

Meanwhile, in a 10-inch skillet, heat oil over moderate heat. Add onions and garlic, and cook until onions are translucent. Stir in tomatoes, basil, oregano, and pepper; raise heat and boil briskly. Cook and stir until mixture becomes a thick puree. Now add puree and squash to beans. Cover and continue cooking over low heat until beans are tender (about 1½–2 hours). When cooking beans, add a little water as needed. When ready to serve, toss corn in and boil hard for last 3 minutes, stirring. Taste for salt and pepper. The beans should be quite thick by this time.

Delicious served with warm flour tortillas. Let people dip from the common bowl with tortillas. Serve a little salsa on the side.

Cheddar Lentils

FEEDS 6 IN JUST UNDER 2 HOURS 30 MINUTES
About 60¢ per serving

1¾ cups dried lentils, rinsed
3½ cups hot water
1 bay leaf
1 teaspoon salt
1 green bell pepper, chopped fine
⅛ teaspoon each of:
    Pepper
    Marjoram
    Sage
    Thyme
2 large onions, peeled and chopped fine
1 1-pound can tomatoes and juice, chopped
    fine
2 cloves garlic, pressed
2 large carrots, sliced into thin rounds
½ cup celery, sliced diagonally
1 cup lowfat cheddar cheese, grated
1 sprig parsley, chopped
(continued)

Preheat oven to 375° F. In a large casserole dish, combine lentils, hot water, bay leaf, salt, bell pepper, spices, onions, tomatoes, and garlic. Cover and bake in preheated oven until lentils are cooked (about 1¼ hours). Remove from oven and stir in carrots and celery. Adjust seasoning. Re-cover and bake an additional 40 minutes or until carrots are soft and cooked through. Stir in half the grated cheese until it melts. Sprinkle remaining half on top, then broil until brown and bubbly (about 5 minutes). Garnish with parsley.

Lima Beans

▼

FEEDS 8 IN 1½–2½ HOURS
About 20¢ per serving

For a complete protein, serve limas with corn bread, corn tortillas, or steamed brown rice.

1 pound dried lima beans
1½ quarts hot tap water
1 teaspoon salt
1 medium onion, minced
¼ cup butter or margarine
4 cloves garlic, minced

Combine water, beans, salt, onions, butter, and garlic in a large saucepan or crockpot. Cook covered over medium-low heat until tender (about 1½ hours in saucepan or 2½ hours in crockpot).

Chile Limas Con Queso

▼

FEEDS 8 IN 2–3 HOURS (45 MINUTES IF BEANS ARE COOKED IN ADVANCE)
About 50¢ per serving

1 recipe Basic Lima Beans, drained (reserve juice)
½ pound fresh green chiles, seeded and sliced thin or 2 4-ounce cans green chiles, drained
1 cup lowfat cheddar cheese, cut into cubes
2 tablespoons olive oil
½ teaspoon sweet basil
¼ teaspoon oregano leaves
½ cup sour cream or yogurt
1 cup reserved bean juice

Preheat oven to 350° F. Spread ⅓ of the drained, cooked beans into a 3-quart casserole. Arrange half the chiles and ⅓ of the cheese over beans. Repeat this step to make a second layer. Then combine olive oil, sweet basil, oregano, sour cream, and 1 cup bean juice. Stir to mix. Pour over all. Top with remaining cheese. Bake uncovered for 30 minutes.

Navy Beans

▼

FEEDS 8 IN 2 HOURS
About 25¢ per serving

1 pound dried navy beans
1 onion, quartered
1 carrot, scrubbed, unpeeled, and
    cut in 2 pieces
½ teaspoon thyme
1 clove garlic, sliced
1 bay leaf
2 cloves
Salt to taste

Combine beans, onion, carrot, thyme, garlic, bay leaf, cloves, and salt in a large saucepan, cover with 2 inches of hot tap water, bring to a boil, then reduce to a simmer, and cook until beans are tender (about 1½ hours). Add water as necessary. Discard bay leaf, onion, carrot, and cloves. Serve as a soup. Delicious with corn bread.

Marinated Bean Salad

▼

FEEDS 8 IN ABOUT 3 HOURS
(INCLUDES MARINATING TIME)
About 55¢ per serving

1 pound dried white, Great Northern, or
    navy beans
Juice of 1 lemon
¼ cup cider vinegar
1 rib of celery, cut fine
½ bell pepper, seeded and chopped
½ medium onion, chopped fine
1 large sprig parsley, chopped, or 2 tablespoons
    dried parsley
Salt and pepper to taste
¼ teaspoon thyme
¾ cup olive oil

Place dried unsoaked beans in 3 quarts of cold, lightly salted water. Bring to boil, then cook gently, adding water as necessary, until just cooked through but not mushy (about 1½ hours). Drain.

In a large salad bowl, combine remaining ingredients and muddle to mix. Add drained beans, mix thoroughly, cover, and refrigerate to marinate about 4 hours or so.

Pasta Fazool

▼

FEEDS 6–8 IN 3–4 HOURS
About 60¢ per serving

1 pound white, Great Northern, or navy beans
1½ quarts hot water
2 medium onions, chopped coarse
2 cloves garlic, pressed
1 tablespoon olive oil
2–3 beef or pork marrow bones
1 8-ounce can tomato sauce
2 cups cooked macaroni or any leftover cooked
    pasta, or ¾ cup uncooked
1 teaspoon rosemary needles
1 tablespoon sugar
Salt and pepper to taste

Cook beans according to package directions. Meanwhile, in a small skillet, sauté onions and (continued) garlic in oil, then add to the cooking beans. Add marrow bones.

Simmer until the beans are soft and done through (1½–3 hours).

Add tomato sauce, macaroni, rosemary, sugar, and salt and pepper to taste. Cook until the macaroni is soft, adding more water if necessary to maintain the consistency of a thick soup.

Remove the bones before serving, knock the marrow out and mash into the soup if you wish. This is one of those soups that ripens and is better the second day.

Pink Beans and Brown Rice

▼

FEEDS 8 IN 3–4 HOURS
About 45¢ per serving

The pink bean is to the pinto as the pheasant is to the chicken. A little drier, a little smoother with a mauve tint. If you like pintos, you will also like pinks. The main difference in taste is that the pinto has an earthy, more pungent flavor than the pink.

Here is another of those peasant dishes that provides complete protein. Essentially a Mexican preparation, it's an attractive dish that is, like most beans and rice dishes, dirt cheap. It also freezes well once it's cooked. This is a good thing to have on hand for those evenings when you can't face anything more than cutting up some radishes.

1 pound dried pink beans or pinto beans
1 onion, chopped coarse
1 clove garlic, minced
2 cloves garlic, chopped
1 teaspoon salt
3–4 strips of bacon or a small piece of salt pork

2 tablespoons olive oil
1 cup brown rice, uncooked
1 onion, peeled and sliced in rings
2½ cups hot reserved bean broth
Cilantro

Rinse unsoaked beans, then place in a large saucepan or crockpot and cover with 2 inches of water. Add onion, half the garlic, salt, and bacon. Bring to a boil, then reduce heat and simmer covered until beans are tender (1½–3 hours). Drain, reserving juice, and set aside. Add water as necessary to maintain level. To cut cooking time for recipe, cook the beans ahead of time.

About 1 hour before serving time, prepare the rice. In a 10-inch skillet, heat olive oil over medium heat until a drop of water sizzles in the skillet. Add rice. Cook and stir until rice begins to brown. Now add sliced onion and remaining garlic and continue stirring until rice grains are golden and beginning to burst. Remove from heat immediately and quickly add hot bean broth. Stir and salt. Cover and simmer until rice is thoroughly cooked and juice is absorbed (about 45 minutes).

When the rice is about ready, check beans and, if necessary, reheat, being careful not to burn the beans on the bottom. Once the rice is cooked, place on a large platter and mound drained cooked beans in the middle. Sprinkle a little cilantro on top. Delicious on a cold winter night with picante sauce or salsa, chopped radishes, cilantro, quartered limes, or avocado strips.

Pinto Beans

▼

FEEDS 8 IN ABOUT 4 HOURS
About 30¢ per serving

1 pound pinto beans
¼ pound salt pork, slashed, or 2–3 strips of
  bacon
1 onion, quartered
Salt to taste
1 tablespoon chili powder (optional)

Combine beans, salt pork, and onion in a medium-large pot. Cover with two inches of water. Bring to a boil over high heat, then reduce heat and simmer until tender, adding water as necessary. The end result is a wonderful bean soup.

Frijoles Refritos

▼

FEEDS 8–10 IN 20 MINUTES
About 35¢ per serving

Mexicans have improved on the old cowboy bean pot by refrying the beans and making a peasant puree of them. You can never get a refried bean dish in a restaurant as good as you can prepare at home. You can cook a whole panful or just a serving or so, depending on how many you have to feed.

2 tablespoons fresh bacon drippings
About 4 cups pinto beans, cooked and drained

Heat drippings in a 10-inch cast-iron skillet over medium-high heat. Add drained beans to skillet. Using a potato masher, mash beans into a coarse puree. Then stir with a big metal spoon and cook, keeping the beans stirred off the bottom of the skillet until you have a fairly dry puree. Remove to a bowl.

Now you have the basis for a bean side dish or a bean chalupa, flauta, or burrito. Refritos served with Spanish rice and a cheese enchilada make a favorite Mexican dinner. Con mucho gusto.

Chalupas Con Frijoles

▼

FEEDS 4 IN 30 MINUTES
About 75¢ per serving

8 corn tortillas
2 tablespoons vegetable oil
2 cups pinto beans, cooked
2–3 tablespoons bacon drippings
Tabasco sauce to taste

6 green onions, chopped fine
2 medium tomatoes, chopped fine
Salt to taste
(continued)

1 large dead-ripe avocado, cut in julienne
*   strips (optional)*
1 cup longhorn or cheddar cheese, grated
Half a head of iceberg lettuce, shredded
Cilantro for garnish
Salsa for garnish

Fry tortillas in very hot oil until golden brown and crisp. Remove to a cookie sheet. In a 10-inch cast-iron skillet, fry cooked pinto beans in bacon drippings over medium-high heat until dry. Season with Tabasco sauce.

Mix onions and tomatoes and salt to taste. Drain well.

Spread about 3 tablespoons of the bean mixture over each tortilla. Press avocado slices into beans. Top with 1 heaping tablespoon of the onion and tomato mixture and then grated cheese. Run under the broiler until cheese begins to brown and bubble. On each serving plate, make a bed of shredded iceberg lettuce and slide two chalupas onto each plate. Serve with a garnish of cilantro and some salsa on the side.

Black Bean Mole

▼

FEEDS 8–10 IN 3 HOURS
About 40¢ per serving

Mole is a spicy sauce made with chiles and usually chocolate and served with meat. Legend has it that nuns invented mole down in Mexico when the Bishop was coming to visit their poor monastery and they had nothing in the larder but a variety of spices and chocolate and one old rooster out in the barnyard.

You can make a wonderful mole without even the benefit of the rooster. Black beans, chili powder, and cocoa. This is a great make-it-on-Sunday and eat it again during the week meal. It freezes well, too. Don't forget some corn bread, tortillas or tortilla chips to accompany. As an added benefit to this Mexican style stew-worth-a-blessing, you'll get zero cholesterol and only a trace of monosaturated fat from the olive oil.

1 pound dried black beans
3 quarts barely salted water
1 rib celery
2 jalapeños, stemmed, seeded, cut in half
2 tablespoons olive oil
1 large yellow onion, coarsely chopped
1 teaspoon sugar
4 cloves garlic, coarsely chopped
1 tablespoon chili powder
1½ tablespoons unsweetened cocoa
3 tablespoons red wine vinegar
Salt and pepper to taste
8 ounces light sour cream or plain nonfat
*   yogurt*
Bunch of cilantro

Cook black beans in boiling water with celery rib and one jalapeño until tender, about 1½ hours. Then spoon out the celery and jalapeño and discard them.

Near the end of the bean cooking, in an 8-inch skillet, heat the olive oil over medium heat. Sauté onion until golden, adding sugar to heighten the color, then add remaining jalapeño and garlic and continue cooking 1 minute. Add chili powder and cocoa and stir to mix about 1 minute. Remove from the heat. Pour vinegar into the mixture and stir, scraping up all the pan drippings. Add this mixture to the beans.

Continue cooking beans 20 minutes more, tasting and adjusting seasonings with salt and pepper. Serve in soup bowls with a dollop of sour cream and fresh cilantro leaves on top.

Navy Beans and Sausage

▼

FEEDS 6 IN 1 HOUR
About 80¢ per serving

Begin with dried beans or canned, make your own impromptu sausage, and serve with applesauce and brown bread for a comforting midwinter meal.

4 cups (2 16-ounce cans) cooked navy beans
1 pound Kielbasa sausage
1 bell pepper, cut into rings

Preheat oven to 350° F. Heat the cooked beans in a casserole dish in the oven (about 15–20 minutes).

Meanwhile, fry sausage in a skillet over medium-high heat; drain. Coil on top of the beans in the casserole dish. Top with green pepper rings. Bake for 15 minutes.

Serve hot in rimmed soup bowls. This recipe tastes better the second day.

Burrito Bake

▼

FEEDS 4 IN 30 MINUTES
About 80¢ per serving

Ever notice how you seem to have 2 flour tortillas left over in the pack after making burritos? And that you only find them curled up, dry, and worthless in the back of the refrigerator, going to waste? Here's a quick and easy one-dish meal that makes the best use of leftover flour tortillas I can think of.

Use canned refried or home-cooked beans you've divided into 2-cup portions to freeze. Two cups of your own homemade pinto beans costs about 10¢. Think of that the next time you crank open a can at 79¢.

You can make this dish ahead up to the baking step. Cover it and keep it in the refrigerator for a day.

If you wish to make the dish look spectacular when serving, shave some iceberg lettuce on the dinner plate, add a wedge of the casserole, then top with fresh tomatoes, a dollop of sour cream or yogurt and black olives.

½ pound lean ground beef
1 medium onion, finely chopped
6 cloves garlic, chopped
¼ teaspoon cayenne pepper
Dash of seasoned salt
½ teaspoon salt
¼ cup water
2 cups refried beans
2 large flour tortillas
(continued)

Optional garnishes:
1¼ cups cheddar cheese, shredded
¼ cup black olives, sliced
2 cups iceberg lettuce, shredded
2 tomatoes, chopped
½ cup plain yogurt

Preheat the oven to 350° F. In a 10-inch skillet over medium-high heat, brown the meat; drain. Add onions, garlic, cayenne, a little seasoned salt, and water to the ground beef. Bring to a boil, then reduce heat and simmer uncovered for 10 minutes. Taste and adjust seasonings if necessary.

Meanwhile, heat refried beans in the microwave for 2 minutes at 100% (HIGH) or in a pan over medium heat for 10 minutes.

Lightly grease a 2-quart round casserole dish. Place 1 tortilla in the bottom of the casserole. Spread the beans over the tortilla, spoon the ground beef mixture over the beans, then layer 1 cup of grated cheese over the beef.

Place the second tortilla over the cheese. Top with remaining grated cheese.

Place the casserole dish in oven and bake until bubbly and the cheese is beginning to brown (about 10–15 minutes).

STREAMLINED LEAN BEANS

Throw away those overly complicated recipes for beans that talk about soaking, and rinsing, and changing waters when cooking beans. Why pour valuable nutrients down the drain? Soak if you must, but cook the beans in the water you soaked in. Why not?

Here's how to make an easy pot of pinto beans to eat and to divide and freeze for impromptu Tex-Mex and Mexican suppers. Remember that beans make a terrific fat-free vegetarian entrée. Protein rich, fiber filled, and always tasty, beans are one old standby whose time has come again.

For flavor, add a chopped onion and a couple of heaping tablespoons of chili powder to the simmering pintos.

Start the beans and water at high heat, then once the water boils, turn the heat down, partially cover the beans and simmer them until the beans are tender. Check the beans from time to time, adding water as necessary to keep it just up over the top of beans. Taste and salt the beans only after they're nearly done. Salted water at the beginning may make the skins tough. Unsoaked pinto beans will cook tender in about 1½ hours. If you presoak them overnight, they're ready in about 1 hour.

Curried Lentil Salad

▼

FEEDS 2 IN LESS THAN 1 HOUR
At just under $1.00 per serving

Lentils are a legume you can cook quicker than any others, with no soaking, no sorting, no fuss whatsoever.

You get solid vegetable protein, a good dose of B vitamins, enough iron to take a shot at anemia, and only the barest whiff of vegetable fat.

Cook at your convenience, drain and refrigerate them, then all you have to do is arrange the dinner on the plate. Even the kids will eat it. And nobody will have too much fat, too much cholesterol, or too much salt. You will have made a good and cheap dinner that's fast and healthy besides.

1 cup dried lentils
1 tablespoon curry powder
2 cups cold tap water
fresh lettuce leaves of your choice
2 cups pineapple chunks, fresh or canned,
*   drained and chilled*
12 red ripe whole strawberries, chilled

Put two dinner-sized plates in the refrigerator to chill. Place in a medium saucepan the lentils, water, and curry powder, and raise to a boil over high heat. Turn the heat down to a simmer and cook just until the lentils are tender, from 30–45 minutes. If the lentils soak up all the water before they're tender, add water a quarter cup at a time and continue cooking until done. Drain and spread out one layer deep to cool in the refrigerator a few minutes.

Serve on a nice white plate covered with ruffled red-tipped lettuce, then discretely tendered with tumeric-hued lentils spiked with pineapple and bordered by delicious strawberries. Yum.

Santa Maria Style Barbecue Beans

▼

FEEDS 12 IN 1½ HOURS
About 40¢ per serving

The pinquito bean is sold in my grocery store under the heading "pink" bean. Basically it's a small pinto bean, that cooks up fairly quickly and has a satisfying slightly sweet, meaty flavor. Remember when cooking this or any other bean to skip soaking or fast soak it (I've just discovered I can do it in the microwave), and don't add salt until the beans are cooked tender.

If beans give you gas, pour the soaking water off, then cook the beans in fresh water. Do know, however, that you are pouring nutrients down the drain when you pour off the soaking water. In cultures where beans are a regular part of the diet, healthy people don't often have problems with intestinal gas. Since we all know that beans are so healthy—they offer soluble fiber, and are an excellent source for protein, iron, vitamins, potassium, and calcium—you should make them a regular part of your diet. Eat them often enough and your system will begin to tolerate the complex sugars that are hard to digest. In other words, if beans give you gas, you're not eating them often enough.

And remember that for economy, the adorable bean can't be beat. A pound of beans, which usually costs less than a dollar, will produce about 10–12 servings. That's about 10¢ apiece before you begin adding other ingredients to the recipe. Beans are one of the best buys you can make for good and cheap cooking.

1 pound dry pinquito beans
6 quarts water
4 slices thick bacon, cut into 1-inch pieces
½ pound lean hamburger
1 large yellow onion, chopped
8 cloves garlic, chopped
1 10-ounce can enchilada sauce, mild or hot
Salt to taste

Rinse beans under running water then soak them in half the water. Place them in the microwave and heat at 100% (HIGH) for 15 minutes. Or, bring them to a boil on the stove, let them boil 2 minutes, then turn off the heat, and let them stand 15–20 minutes.

Meanwhile, in a large soup pot, over medium-high heat, brown the bacon and hamburger meat together until bacon is nearly crisp. Add onion and garlic, and cook and stir until onion is beginning to brown. Now add canned enchilada sauce and cook until it slowly bubbles.

Once the beans have soaked, pour off the water and add them, along with 3 quarts of fresh water, to the soup pot. Bring to a boil over high heat, then lower the temperature and let it bubble slow and uncovered until the beans are tender, about 1½ hours. Taste and add salt if necessary.

Eggs and Cheese

▼

*T*he attraction to eggs is threefold. First of all, for somewhere around 5¢ apiece, eggs are almost pure protein. Second, they are usually there, faithfully reposing in their alabaster apartments ready to yield themselves to the most ambitious experiment. Third, they are quick and easy to cook. In fact, about the only way you can ruin an egg is by overzealous cooking. Crank the heat up too high and the shy little egg will turn to rubber. You've seen women, too adored, whose hearts have turned to stone? So it is with the egg in a smoking skillet.

If you're watching your cholesterol, limit your egg intake to 4 a week. That still leaves lots of room for egg entrées.

I have arranged the recipes according to preparation time—beginning with the simplest, most elegant, and fastest egg dish, the omelet—followed by dishes that take from 10 to 30 minutes. Only the two soufflés require upwards of an hour, and much of that time they spend in the oven.

The egg makes one demand. It will not wait for the diner. Walk the dog after the soufflé comes out of the oven, and the soufflé will collapse in despair. Take out the trash while the huevos are frying, and they'll congeal before you are back in the house. Whenever you serve eggs, observe a certain decorum. Heat the dinner plates and do everything else first, then get the diners to the table on time. Eggs will not disappoint you. It is more a matter of your disappointing them. Carelessly treated, they will shrivel, crackle, retreat. But with proper attention, they will yield themselves to you in perfect abandon.

The Simple Omelet

▼

FEEDS 1 IN 3 MINUTES
About 30¢ per serving

Fancy cookbooks talk about omelets in the most high-flown terms. Yard eggs versus cage eggs. Eggs at room temperature versus refrigerated eggs. Just-laid eggs versus eggs that have been stored. The discussions go on and on.

Then there are interminable discussions of pans. Should the pan be Silverstone? Should it be washed? Should it be reserved exclusively for making omelets? These books have to be kidding.

The truth of the matter is that omelets are good when: (1) you have run out of everything except two dabs of something and a dozen eggs; (2) you are so hungry you cannot possibly wait more than 5 minutes to eat; or (3) you are so tired that you'd rather be shot than have to set foot in the kitchen.

Making an omelet is one of those skills that is too simple to be believed, so people foul it up by making it overly complicated. The first thing to decide is what you plan to fill the omelet with. Heat or prepare the filling first. Set the table first. Do everything first. Make toast. Pour the milk. Put the plate by the stove. The omelet comes together in a hurry and should be served immediately.

You'll need 2 or 3 eggs for each person. Make omelets 1 at a time. Oil the skillet slightly and set it over medium heat. Crack eggs into a small bowl. Add a scant teaspoon of water and a dash of salt and pepper and barely mix with a fork for a striped effect. Pour eggs into the hot skillet and tip to evenly coat the bottom. As the omelet begins to cook, gently run the flat of a fork over the top of it. Lift the edges with a spatula so that raw egg runs underneath.

If the skillet seems too hot, set it aside. You can tell this mostly by smell. If it begins to have that burning hair smell, it's too hot. Once the eggs are about set, remove the skillet from the heat and cover half the omelet with whatever filling you have chosen. Using a spatula, roll the other half of the omelet onto the filled side. Slide the omelet onto the serving dish. A good chef rolls the omelet into a half circle and onto the plate in one smooth motion. If your pan is well seasoned and you work at it, you can learn to do this, too.

The fillings for omelets are limited only by your imagination and your pantry. Fresh sorrel braised in a little margarine then folded into an omelet makes a wonderful dish. Children like glazed apples or browned bananas in their omelets. Almost any leftover sauce, such as marinara, mushroom, or hollandaise, will be good inside the omelet. Plain Parmesan cheese and an extra grating of pepper is good. This list is endless. Growing anything in your garden? Parsley? Fresh tomatoes? Zucchini? Even Mother Hubbard could have made an omelet if she'd just thought about it a few minutes. (continued)

2 or 3 eggs
1 teaspoon water
Salt and pepper to taste
1 teaspoon margarine or butter

Using a fork, barely mix the ingredients together. Melt butter in a 6-inch skillet over medium heat. Pour eggs into pan. Cook, lifting edges so that raw egg runs under. Remove from heat if it gets too hot. Once the top is firm but still shiny and not too wet, remove skillet from fire, add appropriate filling, roll, and turn onto warmed plate.

Lettuce Frittata
▼
FEEDS 4 IN 10 MINUTES
About 30¢ per serving

You can count on the parsimonious French to make use of everything—even wilted lettuce leaves. Here is a lunch that is not only cheap but also blessedly quick. A frittata is an unfolded omelet.

1 tablespoon butter or margarine
2 cups wilted lettuce leaves, any variety
4 eggs
1 tablespoon water
Salt and pepper to taste
½ cup lowfat cheese of your choice, grated
Dash of paprika

Preheat broiler. In a 10-inch skillet heat butter over medium heat. Add lettuce, tearing it into pieces as you drop it into the skillet. Cook and stir for 2 minutes. Beat eggs slightly, then add water and a little salt and pepper. Spread lettuce evenly over the skillet bottom. Reduce heat to medium-low, add eggs to skillet, and cook uncovered over low heat, lifting edges so that raw egg runs under. Once the top is firm but shiny and has no more juicy pockets (no longer than 2 minutes), remove from heat and coat evenly with cheese. Sprinkle generously with paprika and broil until the cheese melts and the top puffs (about 2 minutes).

Serve immediately with hot buttered toast, a piece of fruit, and hot tea. A great lunch and practically free. Moreover, the skillet requires nothing more than wiping out with a paper towel. So you're in and out of the kitchen in 20 minutes.

Kevin's Eggs in Hell

▼

FEEDS 4 IN 10 MINUTES
About 65¢ per serving

A friend goes along as camp cook for a psychologist who takes wealthy wayward teenagers into the wilds to try to transform them from animals to temporary outdoorsmen. The skillet he uses is so enormous that, rather than transport it back and forth each time, he just buries it in the sand at the campsite, digs it up, and cooks supper once they have force-marched these little devils for 15–20 miles through the brush.

1 tablespoon vegetable oil
8 eggs
1 onion, peeled and chopped fine
1 bell pepper, seeded and chopped fine
1 teaspoon chili powder
1 cup chili salsa

8 hot flour tortillas

In a 10-inch cast-iron skillet, heat oil to medium-high. Scramble eggs with other ingredients, except salsa, until eggs are soft-scrambled.

Meanwhile, heat tortillas in a dry skillet 15 seconds to the side. Fold in aluminum foil to keep warm.

When eggs are done, push them to the center of the pan and circle with salsa. Scoop into hot flour tortillas.

Quick Chiles

▼

FEEDS 4 IN 10 MINUTES
About 65¢ per serving

The Mexican campesinos, or peasants, have an intuitive understanding of good nutrition. Here is a peasant dish that provides, in one pan, a complete well-balanced meal. It not only makes use of leftovers but is quick to fix and delicious.

2 slices bacon, chopped
Cooking oil as needed
About 6 stale tortillas, torn into pieces
½ medium onion, peeled and chopped coarse
1 clove garlic, pressed
1 16-ounce can stewed tomatoes with juice, cut
*   coarse, or 2 very ripe fresh tomatoes, chopped*
½ teaspoon salt
1–2 chiles, serranos or jalapeños, seeded and
*   chopped fine (optional)*
1 cup lowfat cheese, grated or thinly sliced

Fry bacon, remove from skillet, and reserve. Add a tablespoon or so of oil, then cook tortillas until crisp. Remove tortillas. Sauté onion and garlic until clear. Put tortillas back in with onions and add tomatoes, salt, and peppers. Cook covered over low heat for 2–3 minutes. Return bacon to the pan. Sprinkle cheese over all, remove from heat, cover, and let stand until cheese is melted.

You can serve this at any time of the day. Try it for breakfast.

Bad Hombre Eggs

▼

FEEDS 4 IN 20 MINUTES
About 65¢ per serving

Toppings:
Juice of ½ lime
1 avocado, peeled, pitted, and sliced
2 tomatoes, sliced thin
4 thin slices purple onion
1 cup longhorn cheese, shredded
Green chili salsa
Salt and pepper to taste
1 tablespoon vegetable oil

4 corn tortillas

1 teaspoon butter or margarine
8 eggs

Preheat oven to 200° F. Warm 4 ovenproof plates.

Meanwhile, squeeze lime juice over avocado. Have avocado, tomatoes, onion, and cheese ready near the stove along with the salsa and salt and pepper.

Heat oil in a 7-inch skillet over medium-high heat. Cook tortillas one at a time, turning once, until lightly brown and crisp. Add oil as needed. Remove to warmed plates. Pour out any remaining oil. Melt butter in skillet and break eggs in 2 at a time. Fry or scramble them, depending on your preference. Remove plates from oven and turn oven to broil. Place cooked eggs on tortillas, salt and pepper to taste, then add toppings. Broil until cheese melts. Serve immediately.

Huevos Rancheros

▼

FEEDS 1 IN 15 MINUTES
About 80¢ per serving

The old ranch egg is good most any time of day. Eat it for breakfast, and you'll start the day singing and dancing "La Cucaracha." Fix it for lunch, and you can have the meal over in moments. Combine it with refried beans for supper and you'll renew your travel visa for Mexico. If you keep the Ranchero Sauce made up in the refrigerator, this dish takes only as long as it takes to fry an egg. This is one of those dinners best made one at a time.

1 corn tortilla
Bacon drippings or butter
2 eggs
Ranchero Sauce (next page)

Preheat oven to 325° F. Heat 1 dinner plate. Meanwhile, in a hot dry skillet, heat tortilla on both sides until it is beginning to crisp (about 20 seconds per side). Remove to hot plate.

Wipe skillet with bacon drippings and fry eggs until the white sets. Slide out onto the tortilla. Cover with a generous portion of warmed Ranchero Sauce and serve immediately.

This dish goes well with a side order of refritos, Spanish rice, guacamole, and papaya for dessert.

Ranchero Sauce

▼

FEEDS 4 IN 20 MINUTES
About 65¢ per serving

Here is the basic sauce for Huevos Rancheros and Chiles Rellenos. It's also good over chicken, meat, or cheese-filled enchiladas.

1 whole onion, chopped
2 bell peppers, seeded and chopped
1 small fresh serrano or jalapeño pepper,
*   seeded and finely chopped*
2 cloves garlic, pressed
1 tablespoon vegetable oil
2 pounds dead-ripe tomatoes or 1 28-ounce
*   can stewed tomatoes*
Salt and pepper to taste

In a 10-inch skillet over medium-high heat, sauté onion, peppers, and garlic in oil until onions are translucent. Run tomatoes through processor or food mill, but leave some texture—no baby food, please. Add tomatoes to onion mixture and simmer until tomatoes are cooked and sauce is slightly thickened. Salt and pepper. This sauce keeps for up to 2 weeks in a covered jar in the refrigerator but should be heated before serving.

Pisto

▼

FEEDS 4 IN 30 MINUTES
About $1.00 per serving

This is where the so-called Spanish omelet began. If you hate shapeless entrées, mound pisto on a crisp tortilla, sprinkle with grated cheddar, and call it migas.

1 thick slice ham (about 6 ounces), diced coarse
1 tablespoon olive oil
1 onion, chopped coarse
1 fresh mild green chile, small jalapeño, or bell
*   pepper, seeded and chopped*
2–3 ripe tomatoes or 1 16-ounce can stewed
*   tomatoes, drained and chopped*
Salt and pepper to taste
6 eggs, well beaten

In a hot dry 10-inch skillet over medium-high heat, fry ham until just beginning to brown on the edges. Remove to plate and reserve. In same skillet, heat oil over medium heat; cook onion and pepper until onion is translucent. Add tomatoes and salt and pepper, replace ham, and simmer for at least 15 minutes to blend flavors. Just before serving, add well-beaten eggs and scramble, taking care to remove the pan from heat while the eggs are still shiny and slightly wet. Serve immediately.

Other things you could add to a pisto are beans, eggplant, potato, and corn. You can also leave out meat altogether or use bacon.

The Spanish Tortilla

▼

FEEDS 4 IN 30 MINUTES
About 40¢ per serving

When Americans visit Spain and order tortillas for lunch, they are surprised to see a sort of omelet being served. This is one of those dishes so simple you can't go wrong, so delicious you will sigh, and so cheap it defies belief.

2 tablespoons olive oil
1 potato, raw, peeled and coarsely grated
1 onion, diced
Paprika
5 eggs
1 tablespoon water
Salt and pepper to taste

In a 10-inch skillet, heat olive oil over medium heat. Add potato and onion, sprinkle generously with paprika, and sauté until onions are translucent and the potatoes are soft and beginning to brown on the edges (about 5 minutes). Stir frequently.

Break eggs into a medium bowl; add water and salt and pepper. Mix gently with a fork (don't overdo this). Once potatoes and onions are cooked, spread them evenly over the bottom of the skillet and pour eggs over. Turn heat to lowest setting, cover, and cook for about 15 minutes, or until brown on the bottom. Meanwhile, preheat broiler, then place skillet under for about 5 minutes to brown the top.

Turn over onto a flat plate so that the crisp brown bottom is on top. The tortilla is good hot, but even better at room temperature. For a party, you can cut the tortilla wedges, spear them with toothpicks, and watch them disappear. For lunch, just serve with a simple green salad and some dry red wine.

Eggs and Onions

▼

FEEDS 4 IN 40 MINUTES
About 50¢ per serving

¼ cup butter or margarine
3–4 medium yellow onions, sliced thin
6 eggs, hard cooked
¼ cup all-purpose white flour
2 cups milk, warmed (in microwave for 1 minute)
Salt and pepper to taste
Hungarian paprika for garnish
Fresh parsley sprigs for garnish

Melt butter in a heavy 5-quart Dutch oven (stainless or porcelain-covered is better than cast-iron) over medium heat. Add onions; cook and stir over medium-low heat until onions lose their shape and become quite translucent (about 25 minutes). Don't brown them. Meanwhile, peel the hard-cooked eggs and cut into ½-inch slices; set aside.

When onions are cooked to a sort of mush, gradually sprinkle in flour, stirring to mix well. Stirring constantly, blend in warmed milk and cook until sauce boils and thickens. Taste and season with salt and pepper. Carefully add egg slices, reserving 6 or so for garnish. Spoon gently onto a large heated rimmed platter. Garnish with remaining egg slices, paprika, and parsley.

Casey's Cream Cheese Soufflé

▼

FEEDS 4 IN 50 MINUTES
About 80¢ per serving

Here is a wonderful egg dish that is as popular with the kids as it is with Daddy. Serve this as a side dish when you have a little leftover roast.

2 3-ounce packages cream cheese, softened in
*   microwave 30 seconds*
⅔ cup (8-ounce carton) sour cream
2 tablespoons honey or molasses
Salt to taste
Dash of cinnamon
4 eggs, separated

Preheat oven to 300° F. Thoroughly mix all ingredients except egg whites. Beat egg whites until stiff, then fold in cheese mixture. Pour into an ungreased soufflé pan, then bake until set (about 45 minutes). Remove when the center just trembles a bit.

When you make this, hope there is a little left that you can eat cold, right out of the pan, the next day for breakfast.

Surefire Cheese Soufflé

▼

FEEDS 4 IN 50 MINUTES
About 60¢ per serving

Soufflés fall for three reasons. First, the cook may overzealously mix the egg yolk sauce into the whipped egg whites, losing too much of the air that has been carefully incorporated. Second, if the soufflé is exposed to a blast of cold air when it is taken from the oven, it may collapse. Third, but most important, if the soufflé is kept for very long before it is served, it will just sigh and retreat back into its dish.

Here is one dinner best served in courses. Get the diners to the table before the soufflé is out of the oven. Serve them a salad and let them wait for the timer's bell to ring. In a moment of high drama, present the perfectly puffed soufflé.

A soufflé is one of the best emergency dinners in any repertoire. No matter how barren the refrigerator is, most people almost always have a carton of eggs and a piece of cheese.

4 tablespoons butter or margarine
5 tablespoons flour
1¼ tablespoons olive oil
1¼ cups milk
Salt and pepper to taste
Paprika to taste
6 eggs, separated
1 cup cheese of your choice, grated

Preheat oven to 350° F. Remove top rack from the oven. Place a cookie sheet on the bottom rack.

In a medium saucepan, make a golden roux of butter and flour over medium heat. Stir in milk. Cook and stir until you have a thick white sauce. Season to taste with salt and pepper and paprika. Set aside to cool to lukewarm.

Beat the egg whites to form stiff peaks. Generously grease a 2-quart baking dish or soufflé dish. Using aluminum foil, make a
(continued)

collar around the dish that stands 3 inches above the top of the dish to act as a reflector to properly brown the soufflé.

Once the white sauce is cool enough so that you can stick your finger in it without being burned, mix in the egg yolks. Stir in cheese. Using a wire whip, make a smooth sauce. Taste and adjust seasonings. You can add a whiff of cayenne pepper if you like. Very gently fold the egg yolk sauce into the whipped egg whites. Don't overdo. Using a rubber spatula, guide the soufflé into the baking dish. Barely smooth the top. If you make a donut-shaped indention on the top of the soufflé, it will rise up in a lovely pattern.

Place the dish on the center of the cookie sheet in oven. Bake without peeking for 30 minutes. At the end of this time, take a look. It should be a golden brown. Tap the dish. If the soufflé trembles, give it 5 minutes or so longer. Remove from oven. Discard foil collar and serve immediately.

Scotch Eggs
▼
FEEDS 6 IN 20 MINUTES
About 35¢ per serving

These eggs make a great pass-back-in-the-car breakfast when you want an early start for a spring break trip.

6 eggs, hard-boiled
1 pound sausage, formed into 6 thin patties

Preheat oven to 350° F. Wrap 1 patty completely around each egg. Place on cookie sheet and bake until sausage is done (about 20 minutes).

Goldenrod Eggs
▼
FEEDS 6 IN 15 MINUTES
About 50¢ per serving

This is the cheapest and best and most cheerful use of abundant Easter eggs. Ask the kids to help by peeling the eggs and making the toast for this festive meal.

6 large eggs, hard-boiled and peeled
2 tablespoons margarine or butter
2 tablespoons flour
Salt and pepper to taste
1 cup milk
Cayenne to taste
6 pieces of buttered toast
Sprig of parsley

Cut the boiled eggs in half, remove the yolks, and mash them. Set aside.

In a medium saucepan, make a thick white sauce by melting the margarine over medium-high heat, then stir in the flour and cook, stirring a few minutes until the flour begins to brown. Add the milk, cook, and stir until sauce thickens. Chop the egg whites into the sauce. Add seasonings.

Meanwhile, place toast on 6 plates. Spoon a serving of sauce onto each piece of toast, then sprinkle the top generously with mashed egg yolk. A sprig of parsley on the plate and soon, you'll have your own Easter breakfast tradition.

Southwestern Egg Bake

▼

FEEDS 6 IN 1 HOUR
About 85¢ per serving

Here's a meal whipped up in 5 minutes then left to bake while you unwind from your workday. Leftover squares make great brown baggers.

1 teaspoon olive oil
1 medium bell pepper (any color), seeded and finely chopped
6 green onions and tops, finely chopped
2 cups lowfat pepper jack cheese, grated
12 large eggs
1 cup milk
8 ounces plain lowfat or nonfat yogurt
¼ teaspoon cayenne pepper
Salt and pepper to taste
Cilantro for garnish
Salsa to accompany

Preheat oven to 350° F. Grease a 9x13-inch glass baking dish with olive oil. Arrange an even layer of bell peppers, then onions, then 1½ cups cheese in the dish.

Whisk the eggs in a large mixing bowl until foamy. Stir in milk, yogurt, salt and peppers and whisk again. Pour the mixture into the bowl. Top with remaining ½ cup cheese.

Bake until puffed, brown, and set (35–45 minutes). Insert a toothpick into the middle of the eggs to see that it comes out clean before removing from the oven. Cool on a rack at least 5 minutes before cutting into squares.

Serve warm or at room temperature topped with cilantro and salsa.

Soups

▼

There's a custom in Louisiana known as lagniappe, the gentle favor a merchant does for a good customer. It's the baker's dozen, the present that's unexpected. Soup is lagniappe for the cook. Whenever you are cooking, there are small gifts—meat drippings, the outer leaves of vegetables—that, if treated with respect, can become the basis of soups to rival those of a fine French restaurant. And many of these treasures are almost free.

Making soup has long been a good and cheap answer to the dinner dilemma. However, the difference in a soup to remember and some watery stew is in the technique.

Take your time making soups. As a general rule, remember that you release sugars in vegetables by sautéing them in the bottom of the soup pot with oil before adding liquids. This is the time to hand-cut and add the vegetables, allowing time for each vegetable to sauté and release its maximum flavor before you add the next one. And since flavor is conveyed in fats, don't leave all the fat out of any soup, or you'll severely compromise the taste.

By the time you are ready to add liquid, you will have a golden brown glaze on the bottom of the soup pot. Add the first liquid a bit at a time, scraping the glaze off the bottom of the pot into solution. This is how you'll get the most out of the soup. Water is the last thing to add.

Soup making is an ancient art. No two pots of one recipe should be alike. Take any soup recipe and make it your own. Substitute some fruit juice for part of the water. Or pour in some beer. Cook and taste and adjust until it suits you. And remember, most soups improve upon standing. A big pot of soup that tastes good the first day, should be better the second and downright divine on the third.

The soup recipes in this chapter fall into four categories: chicken broth, fish stock, red meat stock, and soups and stews. Some outstanding soups are made with water or milk as their base. Some of them are ready in 15 minutes.

Thrifty Chicken Stock

▼

MAKES 1 QUART
About 25¢ a quart

Chicken skin, neck, tail, broken bones, and fat
1 onion, quartered
1 carrot, quartered
1 rib celery, broken in two
1 small pod garlic, crushed
1 peppercorn
1 quart of water

Simmer all ingredients in a medium saucepan uncovered for 1 hour. Taste and add salt, if necessary. The broth should have some body at this point, but needn't taste like a finished soup. Strain, cool quickly, uncovered, then place in a freezer container and freeze. Leave the chicken fat in place. It will preserve the broth and can be used to sauté vegetables in your next recipe.

USING CHICKEN STOCK

Chicken stock can begin with a whole chicken (see Poaching a Chicken, p.48) or with nothing more than skin and bones from a chicken breast that you have boned yourself.

The uses of homemade chicken broth are legion. This is the backbone to my own kitchen, and I use this broth in soups, stews, gravies, and sauces. Rice and pasta cooked in broth are divine. I never hesitate to use chicken stock in a new recipe that might call for beef stock when I have no beef stock.

In any of the recipes here calling for chicken stock, canned chicken broth will work. But it is really salty and may contain monosodium glutamate to boot, so if you are beginning with a commercial broth, taste soup carefully before adding more salt. And when you open that can of broth, take a long look at the price marked on the top of the can. That's a lot of money for a can of flavored water.

Tortilla Soup

▼

FEEDS 4 IN 20 MINUTES
About 40¢ per serving

Here is a Mexican peasant soup that is both filling and wonderful.

2 tablespoons cooking oil
2 onions, cut into chunks
3 garlic cloves, chopped fine
1 bell pepper, cut into julienne strips
3–4 ripe tomatoes, chopped
4 cups chicken broth
½ teaspoon cumin seed
Salt and pepper to taste
⅔ cup cheese (jack, mozzarella, or cheddar), grated
5–6 stale tortillas, torn into pieces

In a medium saucepan, heat oil over medium-high heat. Sauté onion, garlic, and bell pepper until onion is translucent. Add tomatoes and (continued) cook a minute or so to thicken the base. Now add broth and bring to a boil.

Meanwhile, if your tortillas are fresh, dry them in a hot oven or in a skillet. Cool and tear into pieces.

Once the broth is boiling, add cumin and salt and pepper. Reduce heat and stir in cheese. Do not boil. At the last instant, stir in tortillas. Serve in a rough earthenware tureen if you have one.

HOW TO MAKE A ROUX

In many places in this book, I have simply said, make a roux. A roux is flour and fat cooked together as a thickening agent for soup, sauce, or gravy, not always in equal amounts, though. Sauce can be thin, medium, or thick. The flour proportion adjusts accordingly. As a guideline:

1 part flour to 2(½) parts fat = thin
1 part flour to 1 part fat = medium
2 parts flour to 1 part fat = thick

Here are the detailed instructions for making a roux:

In a heavy skillet, place equal parts oil or shortening and flour. Over medium-low heat, stirring constantly, cook and stir this mixture until it has cooked to a deep, rich, walnut-brown color. The smell and color of this roux will change as it goes along. At first, when it's the palest amber hue, it will have a raw-flour smell, a kind of wallpaper-paste aroma. As you cook and stir, the aroma will deepen and become more robust and more like that of some baked goods you've had in the oven that were on the verge of burning. That's the cooked-flour smell. The secret to making a roux is to cook the flour and oil until the last instant before it burns, then to cool down the mixture with chopped vegetables that are stirred in vigorously. If only we could know who the brilliant cook was who figured this out—what a technique! What an inimitable result. There are no shortcuts (don't mention those microwave directions for making a roux—the eighth deadly sin), but the resulting stew is so good you'll want it once a week.

M—M—GOOD CREAM GRAVY

I will be the first to tell you that the art of making a good cream gravy seems to have gone along the same route as that of making hand-split cedar shingles—not enough people know how any more. However, if you can master cream gravy and then combine it with a decent batch of cornmeal mush, you will be on your way to a grain-based entrée that is both good and cheap.

The secret to making cream gravy is to start with a black cast-iron skillet. Melt the fat—butter or oil or drippings—in the skillet over medium-high heat, stir in an equal amount of flour and cook and stir until the roux looks bubbly and you can smell the aroma of cooked flour. Then dribble in the milk, stirring vigorously and constantly, keeping the heat at a simmer. As soon as the mixture boils and thickens, season to taste with salt and pepper. I often add a shot of cayenne to heighten the taste. Now tell me that's not good. And done properly, the only lump will be in your throat because it reminds you of your mama.

Frugal Asparagus Soup

▼

FEEDS 4 IN ABOUT 15 MINUTES
About 10¢ per serving (almost a free lunch)

This is offered not so much as a specific recipe but as an attitude toward foods on hand. Leftovers from a simple roast chicken dinner can be used to make a delicious soup, i.e., pan drippings, a little hollandaise, woody asparagus stalks.

Here is how these three elements combined to make a soup fit for the gods:

First, I steamed the asparagus stalks just until tender. Meanwhile, I made a roux in a saucepan. When it was cooked, I added a couple of tablespoons of the chicken gelatin and stirred it vigorously. At this point, it looked like the basis for some sort of pudding. Then I thinned it with some milk, stirred it until it was lump-free, then left it to simmer while I turned my attention back to the stalks.

I ran the tender steamed stalks through the food mill, tossing in a couple of tablespoons of leftover hollandaise, hoping for a nice puree. The woody shards were left in the mill. It looked like too much of the good stuff wasting on the inside of the sieve, so I poured some milk through it. Once I was through rubbing the back of a big spoon around the inside of the mill, there was little but wood left inside. The lovely pale green puree was all in the pot.

Now I stirred the soup thoroughly, added a little more milk because it seemed too thick, and when I had it just the consistency of a nice cream soup, I tasted it for the first time. It was too good to be true—as soft as velvet, as subtle as a fine French wine.

So what did this lunch cost? Can you count asparagus stalks—a throwaway? Can you count pan drippings from the chicken? Usually the dog gets these. The hollandaise? There wasn't enough left over to use it again in its original state. So this brings us down to several cups of milk, some flour, and some margarine. No more than 40 cents any way you cut it—10¢ a serving—and the soup fed four people in such an admirable way that we were thunderstruck.

Time? It was all done in about 15 minutes. Additives? None. Salt? Very little. Texture? Equal to the finest pure cream soup, although it was made solely with milk. We ate extravagantly well, with fewer calories, less cost, and less trouble than such a fancy soup made from scratch would suggest. To my mind, this is true economy.

Woody stalks from a pound of asparagus
2 tablespoons hollandaise
(continued)

Roux:
1½ tablespoons flour
1½ tablespoons margarine or oil
3 cups milk
2 tablespoons chicken drippings (mostly gelatin)
Dash of cayenne pepper
Salt to taste

Steam asparagus stalks until tender (about 7 minutes in the microwave or 15 minutes on the stove).

Make a roux from flour and margarine or oil. When golden, add chicken gelatin and stir until it looks shiny. Thin with milk.

Process stalks with hollandaise in food mill, then pour milk through one sieve to force remaining puree into the soup.

Stir and heat to boiling. Taste for seasoning. Give it a dash of cayenne pepper; salt if you must. Serve immediately.

VEGETABLE CREAM SOUP

Here is a basic procedure for making a vegetable cream soup from humble beginnings. You can use one vegetable alone or more vegetables in combination. Precook all vegetables except the leafy ones before combining them with the cream sauce. If you wish to give it a French finish, then puree the vegetables once you have precooked them. Sautéing finely chopped or grated vegetables in butter or margarine makes for a nice soup. If you're making soup from leftover vegetables, knock 10 minutes off the preparation time and proceed to make the cream sauce. Choose whatever seasonings you usually like with that particular vegetable in other dishes.

The possibilities for cream vegetable soups are as extensive as the vegetables you have in your refrigerator or pantry. Any of the following can be made into a lovely soup: watercress, spinach, chard, pumpkin, onions, carrots, zucchini, parsnips, potatoes, celery, squash of all sorts, mushrooms, broccoli, leeks, and even lowly lettuce. You don't have to have picture-perfect vegetables for soup. I've made some decent soups from some pretty pitiful looking carrots. Just taste the raw vegetable. If the vegetable is good, the soup will be good.

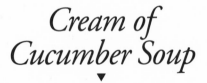

Cream of Cucumber Soup

▼

FEEDS 4 IN 30 MINUTES
About 30¢ per serving

1 cucumber, unpeeled
3 tablespoons butter or margarine
2 tablespoons flour
2 cups milk
2 cups chicken stock
1 teaspoon dill
Salt and pepper to taste
1 tablespoon sherry (optional)

Grate cucumber; if not young and tender, remove seeds. Sauté in a small skillet over medium heat in 1 tablespoon of the butter until tender (about 10 minutes). In a soup pot, make a golden roux from the remaining 2 tablespoons butter and flour. Make a thick cream sauce with the remaining ingredients. Stir in cucumber. Simmer for 10 minutes, but do not boil. Taste and adjust seasonings. Stir in sherry and serve.

Zucchini Soup

▼

FEEDS 4 IN 30 MINUTES
About 25¢ per serving

With a homegrown zucchini grande and a lemon, you have the basis for a quick, delicious soup that costs almost nothing and is very easy to make. This is a fresh, astringent summer soup, flecked with yellow and green.

2 cups grated zucchini
Juice of 1 lemon
2 cups chicken broth
1 tablespoon cooking oil
1 onion, chopped
2 cloves garlic, pressed
Salt and pepper to taste

In medium saucepan combine zucchini, lemon juice, and broth. Raise to a boil. Meanwhile, in a 7-inch skillet, heat oil on medium-high and sauté onion and garlic until onion begins to brown. Now combine with zucchini. Salt and pepper to taste. Boil gently for 10 minutes.

Peas-Porridge Hot

▼

FEEDS 8–10 IN 1 HOUR 30 MINUTES
About 30¢ per serving

This recipe is the result of one of those happy accidents that came about trying to substitute yellow split peas for navy beans in Navy Bean Salad. It looked absolutely unappetizing, but with some chicken broth and a stew pot and 15 minutes' boiling time, necessity became the mother of invention and a new soup recipe was developed.

1 pound dried yellow split peas
Juice of 1 lemon
¼ cup cider vinegar
1 rib of celery, cut fine
½ bell pepper, chopped
½ medium onion, chopped fine
¼ cup parsley, chopped
Salt and pepper to taste
¼ teaspoon thyme
2 cups chicken broth

Place dried peas in large soup pot with 3 quarts cold, lightly salted water. Bring to a boil, cooking gently until just cooked through—a little less than 1 hour. Drain. Add remaining ingredients to soup pot and boil gently until thick and smooth and delicious (about 15 minutes). If using canned broth, be careful not to oversalt.

Fish Stock

▼

MAKES 1 QUART IN ABOUT 45 MINUTES
About 50¢

When it comes to making fish stock, there's
good news and bad news. The good news is
that this is as easy as making chicken stock and
can provide a surprise underpinning to soups
and sauces that will render the product more
complex and interesting than you might have
imagined. The bad news is that for the 30
minutes you simmer the fish stock, your entire
house may smell like the back door of a sec-
ond-rate fish market.

Only make fish stock to prepare a soup that
you want somebody to remember. Fish stock
in plain potato soup, or vichyssoise, will ele-
vate the humble potato to a sublime station.
Using cold fish stock in the gazpacho recipe
instead of all tomato juice will make you hum
"Granada."

2 pounds fresh fish heads, bones, skin,
 trimmings, and shells
1 cup dry white wine (preferably vermouth)
½ large onion, sliced
½ large carrot, sliced
1 small clove garlic, crushed
2–3 peppercorns
Bay leaf
Salt to taste

Place all ingredients in a medium-large
saucepan and add water to cover. Simmer
uncovered for about 30 minutes. At the end of
this time, taste and adjust salt. Strain and
freeze.

Vichyssoise Del Mar

▼

FEEDS 6 IN 1 HOUR
About 35¢ per serving

2 large yellow onions, sliced thin
2 tablespoons olive oil
4 medium potatoes, peeled and chopped coarse
2 cups fish stock
2 tablespoons butter or margarine
2 tablespoons flour
3 cups milk
Salt and pepper to taste
Parsley, chives, or green onion tops for garnish

In a medium-sized saucepan, sauté onions in oil over low heat for at least 15 minutes or until the onions have cooked down to a limp, caramel-colored mass. Now add potatoes and fish stock and boil gently until potatoes are tender (about 30 minutes). Using a potato masher or food mill, make a smooth puree of this mixture.

   Meanwhile, in a small skillet, make a golden roux from butter and flour, then combine with pureed potatoes. Add milk and heat thoroughly, whipping with a wire whisk to smooth puree. Season to taste with salt and pepper. Serve garnished either hot or cold. If you plan to serve this cold, as a true vichyssoise, be bold with the seasonings, for chilling tames the salt and pepper.

Quick Fish Chowder

▼

FEEDS 4 IN 30 MINUTES
About 75¢ per serving

Use frozen fish or today's catch. It's quick. Easy. Cheap.

3 tablespoons olive oil
¾ cup onion, chopped
2 ribs celery, sliced
1 teaspoon chili powder
1 pound stewed tomatoes
1 cup water or fish stock
1 teaspoon salt
1 teaspoon sugar
1 teaspoon Worcestershire sauce
1 pound of fish, fresh or frozen, cut into bite-sized chunks
Parsley or cilantro for garnish
1 cup rice, uncooked

Heat olive oil in a heavy saucepan over medium heat. Add onion, celery, and chili powder. Sauté for 10 minutes. Stir in tomatoes, water, salt, sugar, and Worcestershire sauce; bring to a rolling boil. Add fish to boiling mixture. Lower heat and simmer uncovered for 15 minutes.

   Meanwhile, cook rice according to package directions. Serve over rice and sprinkle with parsley or cilantro.

Sopa De Ajo

▼

FEEDS 4 IN 30 MINUTES
About 15¢ per serving

The Spanish have come the closest to making an edible stone soup, except the Spanish stone is garlic. You can make this soup with beef, fish, or chicken stock or, as a last-ditch effort, with plain water. Spaniards eat this soup when dieting because it is satisfying, yet low in calories and fats.

3 tablespoons olive oil
5 cloves garlic, sliced thin
4 slices stale bread
1 teaspoon paprika
5 cups broth or hot water
2 eggs
Salt and pepper to taste
Lime slices for garnish (optional)
Cilantro for garnish (optional)

Preheat oven to 450° F. In a medium soup pot, heat olive oil almost to the smoking point. Sauté sliced garlic until golden, then the bread slices—brown on both sides over high heat, taking care not to burn. Remove toasted bread to ovenproof casserole dish or tureen. Remove soup pot from heat and add paprika, stirring to mix with any remaining oil. Pour broth or water into soup pot, replace bread, and bring to a boil. Salt and pepper to taste. As bread softens and swells, break it apart using two spoons.

Cover and cook for 15–20 minutes.

About 5 minutes before you are ready to serve, beat eggs until lemon-colored. Pour soup into tureen and carefully spread eggs over the surface of the soup. Bake uncovered in preheated oven until a brown crust forms (about 5 minutes). Alternately, you can poach the eggs in the soup.

Serve with lime slices and a sprinkling of cilantro.

Beef Stock

▼

MAKES 1 GALLON IN 4–6 HOURS
About 75¢

Butchers used to give away bones for the dog, but no more. Today, the going rate is almost a dollar a pound. If you decide to try a homemade beef stock, look for bones with marrow. Plan to make the stock when you're going to be home at least half the day. Making stock takes time—not much attention, but a good bit of time. However, the job is worth it just for that earthy smell the kitchen takes on as the stock develops.

3–4 pounds cracked beef, veal, and/or pork
  bones with marrow
2 carrots, sliced
4 onions, sliced
1 teaspoon sugar
Fresh-ground pepper
1 turnip, sliced
1 stalk celery, sliced
1 bay leaf
3–4 peppercorns
Salt to taste

Preheat oven to 425° F. Place bones in a large Dutch oven and cook uncovered in the hot oven for 1 hour, turning once or twice. Add half the carrots and onions, sprinkle sugar and pepper over all, and continue cooking in hot oven 1 more hour.

Remove to stove top. Cover well with cold water, then add remaining ingredients. Bring to a boil, scraping sides of pan to incorporate the caramelized essences. Simmer about 3 hours. Taste and adjust seasoning. Strain and freeze.

Basic Beef Stew
▼
FEEDS 8 IN ABOUT 2 HOURS
About 45¢ per serving

Buying beef requires the shrewdness of a diamond merchant—there are many cuts, all with different names. It's a cinch that if you are on a limited budget you won't be ordering T-bones. But does this mean hamburger is your only alternative? Ounce for ounce you may be able to provide more meat by choosing other cuts.

On one visit to my market, hamburger was selling at $2.19 per pound. Boneless stew meat was a staggering $3.59; but my old friend, chuck roast, was on sale for $1.29. A 6-pound chuck roast, cut into three 2-pound pieces provided three meals for our family of four with a bone left over to make stock. I processed a portion into ground chuck, which was much redder and with a lower fat ratio than the higher-priced hamburger at the market. The second portion I cut into stew meat, and the third became a small but succulent pot roast. Of the three choices, the stew meat produced the most satisfying meal—the delicious stew recorded here.

2 pounds chuck roast, cut into chunks
2 tablespoons beef fat
Flour
Salt and pepper
½ pound fresh mushrooms, sliced
3 yellow onions, chopped
2 cloves garlic, pressed
2 teaspoons dill
½ teaspoon basil
½ teaspoon thyme
½ teaspoon savory
1 bay leaf, crushed
4 cups beef broth (homemade canned, or bouillon cubes)
1 pound carrots, scraped and cut into chunks
2 cups raw pasta, rice, or potatoes

Trim fat from chuck roast and place it in a large roasting pan. Over medium-low heat, render fat. When fat pieces are brown and crisp, remove. Make a total of 2 tablespoons of fat in the roaster.

Dredge meat chunks in flour seasoned with salt and pepper; brown on all sides in the fat. Add mushrooms, onions, garlic, dill, basil, thyme, savory, and bay leaf. Sauté slowly until onions are clear and beginning to turn golden (about 25 minutes). Then add broth and carrots. Cover and simmer gently until the meat is tender (about 1½ hours). Adjust seasonings.

Near the end of the cooking time, in a separate pan, cook pasta, rice, or potatoes in boiling salted water. Then place a big spoonful in a bowl and cover with stew. Garnish with parsley.

This stew freezes well, but don't combine it with the pasta or rice before freezing.

Zorba's Stew

▼

FEEDS 4 IN 2 HOURS
About 85¢ per serving

This recipe is method over all. You can make a good version of this stew by substituting equal amounts of okra or zucchini for the eggplant.

2 small eggplants
2 onions, chopped coarse
1 tablespoon olive oil
1 tablespoon margarine
1 pound lamb stew meat with bones (neck is
*   good)*
1 pound boneless veal stew meat
3 garlic cloves, sliced
1 cup dry white wine
Salt and pepper to taste
¼ cup parsley, chopped
1 cup beef broth

Cut eggplants into large pieces, about 6 per eggplant. Salt well and let them stand about 30 minutes in colander to draw out the juices.

In a large flameproof casserole over medium heat, sauté onions in olive oil and margarine until translucent. Add meat and garlic, cooking until golden brown on all sides. Add wine and gently season with salt and pepper. Cover and reduce heat; let simmer for 30 minutes.

Meanwhile, wash and dry eggplant pieces. In a lightly oiled 10-inch skillet, brown the eggplant. Add eggplant, parsley, and broth to meat; cover and simmer slowly for about 1 hour or until eggplant is limp but not mushy. Taste and adjust seasoning.

Instant Tomato Soup

▼

FEEDS 2 IN 10 MINUTES
About 25¢ per serving

Here is a soup that requires no stock, and is quick besides. In fact, this is an almost instant soup.

1 7-ounce can tomato sauce
2 cups milk
1 tablespoon butter or margarine
Parmesan cheese
Salt and pepper to taste

In a saucepan heat tomato sauce and milk to just below the boiling point. Stir in butter, add salt and pepper, and garnish with Parmesan cheese. Who needs a can of tomato soup?

Mulligatawny

▼

FEEDS 8 IN 1 HOUR
About 50¢ per serving

One week I was cleaning out the refrigerator and started soup with some limp, tired vegetables that weren't much good for anything else. I'd started by doing what I always do to make soup: slowly sautéing vegetables in the bottom of a big pot.

You think the French revive fond memories dipping a cookie into hot tea. Take a whiff from a pan of sizzling vegetables and see what pops into your head. I get ideas just inhaling the sweet, pungent aroma of caramelizing onions and garlic.

I had started with onions—a handful of little boilers that were beginning to sprout. Then I'd chipped in some celery so limber it looked like wet spaghetti. Then some garlic, a carrot, one green apple, and a handful of mushrooms. Sprinkled a pinch of sugar and grated some pepper over all and that's when curry came to mind.

Indians get the most flavor from spices by frying them in butter first. So, while I still had a little oil in the bottom of the pot, I threw in curry powder—generously—and stirred. Next I browned one lone chicken breast found lurking in the freezer door.

What I'd backed into is known as mulligatawny, an English vegetable soup as interpreted by East Indian cooks. It just shows what you can do with common ingredients and dry spices. To add the finishing touch, I pureed it all in a food processor, added cream, and served

each bowl with a sprig of cilantro and a dollop of plain yogurt.

2 tablespoons vegetable oil
4 cups fresh raw vegetables, coarsely cut:
Onions
Garlic
Carrots
Celery
Parsnips
Potatoes
Mushrooms
1 green apple, peeled, cored and chopped
½ teaspoon sugar
2 tablespoons curry powder
½ teaspoon cayenne pepper
½ teaspoon pepper
1 cup chicken meat, lamb or beef (optional)
3 tablespoons flour
4 cups broth (chicken, beef, or vegetable)
1 cup rice, cooked
½ cup heavy cream or peanut butter or coconut milk
Cilantro for garnish
Plain lowfat yogurt for garnish

Sauté the vegetables in hot oil in a soup pot over medium-high heat, adding them one by one as you cut them, beginning with the onions and garlic, then adding in order those that will take the longest to cook. Add apple and sugar, stirring to caramelize. Stir in curry powder and peppers and fry for 2 minutes. Add meat if you wish and brown. Stir in flour. Cook and stir about 2 minutes.

Add broth, stir and simmer until the vegetables are soft, about 30 minutes. Add cooked rice. Lift cooked vegetables and meat from the broth and puree in food processor or food mill, return mixture to the broth, and adjust seasonings.

Finish soup with cream, peanut butter or coconut milk. Serve hot in soup bowls with a cilantro sprig and a dollop of yogurt floating atop.

Polish Treat

▼

FEEDS 6 IN 1 HOUR
About 59¢ per serving

The peasant wisdom of using a little meat and a lot of vegetables together to make up a wholesome dinner that not only is good for you but tastes good too, shows in this old-country Polish recipe.

Keep the water level barely above the potatoes—don't make this into some sort of thin Dickensish broth. The rich flavor of vegetables and sausage simmered together into a perfumed stew will keep them coming back for more.

The general rule of thumb when making this or any other ad lib stew is that you should cook and taste, adjusting the seasonings as you go.

6 medium potatoes, peeled and coarsely chopped
6 medium carrots, scraped and cut into 1–2
  inch pieces
6 onions, peeled and quartered
1 pound kielbasa sausage, cut into 2-inch pieces
1 medium head cabbage, cored and cut into six
  wedges
Salt and pepper to taste
Butter or margarine to taste

Place potatoes and carrots in a soup pot with water to barely cover. Bring to a boil, then cover the pot, reduce the heat, and simmer until the vegetables are barely tender, about 10 minutes. Add onions, sausage, and cabbage, and salt and pepper. Cover and simmer until the cabbage is soft, about 15 minutes. Adjust seasonings and serve with a little butter or margarine for an easy, delicious, good and cheap dinner.

Cool Gazpacho

▼

FEEDS 6 IN 20 MINUTES
PLUS 1 HOUR TO CHILL
About 50¢ per serving

1 cup water
2 slices soft white bread
1 tablespoon Tarragon vinegar
2 cloves garlic
Salt and pepper to taste
Cayenne to taste
1 28-ounce can plum tomatoes
¼ cup olive oil
½ teaspoon sugar
Bell pepper for garnish

Soak the bread in the water in a shallow dish. Add vinegar, garlic, salt and pepper, and cayenne. Set aside.

Cook the tomatoes in olive oil with the sugar in a 10-inch skillet over medium heat about 8 minutes or until they're thickened.

Blend bread and tomato mixtures in the blender thoroughly. Add 4 ice cubes. Refrigerate until chilled.

Serve in consomme bowls, garnished with chopped bell pepper.

Caldo Verde

▼

¼ cup olive oil
6 cloves garlic, peeled and mashed
1 medium leek with 2-inches of green, chopped,
    or 1 medium onion
½ teaspoon sugar
4 medium russet potatoes, scrubbed and
    chopped (leave skins on)
1 pound link linguica, chorizo, or other link
    sausage (optional)
4 cups chicken or vegetable broth
1 bunch kale or collards, shredded
Salt and pepper to taste

Heat a large soup pot over medium heat dry, then add olive oil. Add garlic and leek and sauté until the vegetables begin to brown. Sprinkle with sugar and keep cooking and stirring, scraping the bottom of the pan. Add potatoes and cook, stirring until they begin to brown (about 5 minutes).

Then add sausage and sauté until brown. Pour in the broth and add enough water to cover by about 1 inch. Raise the soup to a boil. Scrape the bottom of the pan to release the browned bits into the soup. Simmer until the sausage is cooked through and the potatoes are tender, about 15 minutes.

Drop in the shredded kale and simmer an additional 5 minutes or until the ribs of the greens are tender.

Adjust seasonings and serve piping hot over thick slices of French or brown bread.

Farmer's Market Chili

▼

A little kick in the chili is good, but I do hate the bite traditional chili takes when I add up the costs. The easy way out—buying chili in cans—shocks me when I see that each can costs upwards of a dollar.

Factor into that enough fat and cholesterol to make your vessels slam shut, and you've got the story on most meat-based chilies. But this chili is based on the garden. Made with olive oil, it has only ¼ cup for 32 servings, or a mere 1.625 grams of monosaturated fat at 14 calories in each serving. And let me tell you, it is good, as well as good for you!

1 cup navy beans, dry
1 cup red kidney beans, dry
1 30-ounce can chili beans and juice
¼ cup olive oil
2 eggplants, coarsely chopped
2 large yellow onions, coarsely chopped
6 cloves garlic, minced
2 medium zucchini, coarsely chopped
1 large bell pepper, seeded and diced

2–3 jalapeño peppers, seeded and minced
3 pounds Roma tomatoes, coarsely chopped or 3
    16-ounce cans, with juice
2 tablespoons chili powder
1 tablespoon whole cumin seeds
1 teaspoon dried oregano
Salt and pepper to taste
(continued)

Garnishes (optional):
Cilantro
Green onions, chopped
Tomatoes, minced
Longhorn or cheddar cheese, grated
Sour cream or plain nonfat yogurt

Cover navy beans and kidney beans with one inch of salted water in a medium saucepan and parboil about 45 minutes. Add canned chili beans and continue to cook.

Meanwhile, heat a large soup pot over medium-high heat and add oil. Add vegetables one at a time to the hot oil. Take your time, giving each vegetable time to sauté. Stir, but keep the heat up so that vegetables will begin to brown.

After 30 minutes or so, when the vegetables have begun to cook down, add remaining spices. Cook a few more minutes, then pour in beans.

Turn the heat down to medium-low and let the chili simmer uncovered for 2–3 hours, stirring occasionally. Add water as needed to maintain a soupy consistency.

Cover and let the chili stand until it reaches room temperature. Adjust seasonings. You can reheat and serve it now, or you can freeze.

Serve each bowl with a garnish of choice.

Breads and Desserts

▼

Now I'm not about to sit here and tell you that you'll save money if you make all your own yeast bread at home. You know that already. Just to remind you, a 1½-pound loaf of homemade white bread costs less than 50¢. And hot out of the oven it tastes so good that should your family get addicted to it, as ours has, they may not permit you to buy that awful white fish-food bread from the supermarket. Not even hot out of the corporate oven. Even fresh, at full price, commercial white bread is still not good for anything but picking up broken glass. But you can find a recipe for plain homemade yeast bread in any general cookbook. I want to share with you some luxury breads and down-home quick breads you can make that are both good and cheap.

The nutritious desserts in this chapter are based on fruit, or cheese, or eggs, or milk. At the end are a couple of easy cookies, and a crunchy dessert based on oats. Enjoy!

HOMEMADE BREAD

I am constantly amazed at the price of best-quality bakery bread. Somebody sent me a price list from a real good Italian bakery in Houston. Plain sourdough baguettes were priced at $4 and with the addition of anything else—pistachio apricot, lemon herb, or even whole wheat—the price jumped to $5. That's pretty staggering for a one-pound loaf, when you consider that you could make the same thing at home for about 50¢ for a baguette of plain bread. Add the cost of other ingredients and I dare say it would never touch the dollar mark, even if you added a handful of high-priced pistachios and dried apricots.

In my opinion, the best good and cheap grub you can make is that which competes favorably with luxury comestibles. Of course, you can save money buying day-old bread. So what? It's still inferior commercial bread—only on its way to a desiccated descent into processed dinner hell.

When writing *Bread in Half the Time*, we learned some tricks of the baker's trade. For example, you can get a pretty fair approximation of sourdough by adding a half cup of rye flour to 3 cups of bread flour.

To create those gorgeous finishes that make the bread look like it's dusted with toasted flour and straight from the fanciest bakery on the Upper East Side, all you do is rub whole-wheat flour into a clean terry cloth washcloth that you're willing to keep in the kitchen. Fold the cloth with the flour on the inside, place it in a sealable plastic bag and keep it handy for baking days. Once the dough is formed for the final rise, unfold the cloth and place it, floured side down, on the dough while it rises. Once the dough has risen to almost double in bulk, carefully remove the washcloth. Cut deep slashes at a 45-degree angle into the top of the loaf (it should spring open as you cut since the yeast has already worked). Pop the bread into the hot oven. Once it's baked, the flour will have toasted on top and the slashes that didn't have flour in them will stand out in dramatic relief. Easy huh?

You can make bread in several ways. Make it in my 1½-pound bread machine, using the dough setting, or in the food processor and raise it in the microwave. Last but not least, hand-knead bread and raise it in a warm, draft-free place. You can make it any way that suits you. Always remember to hand-knead when adding fruits and nuts. Machines tend not only to knead them in but to chew them up and practically digest them before you even get the bread into the oven.

Raisin Rosemary Bread

▼

MAKES A 1-POUND LOAF
IN 1½ HOURS
About $1.00

2 cups bread flour
½ cup rye flour
¼ cup yellow cornmeal
1 cup whole-wheat flour
2½ teaspoons (1 packet) 50%-faster active
    dry yeast
1 tablespoon sugar
1 teaspoon salt
¾ teaspoon black pepper, coarse ground
⅓ cup powdered milk
2 tablespoons olive oil
1½ cups warm water (110° F)
1 cup raisins (optional)
1 cup walnuts (optional)
2 tablespoons rosemary needles (optional)

Fit the food processor with the steel blade. Put all dry ingredients in the work bowl and pulse to aerate and mix.

With the motor running, pour in the olive oil and warm water, holding back the last tablespoon or so of water. Process until the mixture forms a ball that cleans the sides of the bowl. Add the last bit of water if needed to make a soft dough. Machine knead for 60 seconds, then knead in the raisins, walnuts, and rosemary by hand on a lightly floured surface.

You can raise the dough in the food processor work bowl easily. Punch a hole in the center of the dough ball making a donut shape and drop it back into the work bowl. Cover with plastic wrap. Let rise in a warm, draft-free place until doubled in bulk, or micro-rise in your 500-watt or higher microwave.

Remove the dough to a lightly floured surface and punch it down. Cover the dough with the work bowl and let it stand 10 minutes. Meanwhile, preheat the oven to 400° F.

Grease a 9-inch glass pie plate. Form the dough into a ball and place it in the pan. Cover with a washcloth you've rubbed whole wheat flour into. Raise the dough until almost double in bulk again.

Remove the floured cloth, cut deep zig-zag slashes in the top of the loaf using a razor blade, then pop into the oven and bake about 50 minutes, until it's golden on the top and sounds hollow when tapped on the bottom.

Cool on a rack before slicing. Cut the loaf into two pieces, then place the cut side down, and cut thick slices from each half.

HOW TO MICRO-RISE DOUGH

To micro-rise, lower microwave setting to 10% power, place an 8 ounce glass of water in the back, then add the dough in the processor bowl. Heat 3 minutes, rest 3 minutes, heat 3 minutes, and rest 6 minutes. Dough will now be doubled in bulk.

Skillet Potato Bread

▼

MAKES A 3-POUND LOAF
IN ABOUT 3 HOURS
About 60¢ per loaf

The next time you are asked to contribute to a communal supper, want to provide something dramatic, and haven't but 65¢ to spare, volunteer to bring this loaf of potato bread. Baked in a 10-inch cast-iron skillet, this pungent loaf of bread will easily serve a dozen or more people, has a good close grain that makes it ideal for sandwiches, is better the second day, and—in terms of bread making—is quite easy.

1 cup mashed potatoes
1 tablespoon active dry yeast
2½ cups warm water
3 tablespoons flour
2 tablespoons sugar
8 cups all-purpose flour
2 tablespoons salt

Preheat oven to 95° F, then turn oven off. Meanwhile, in a medium mixing bowl combine yeast with ½ cup warm water, 3 tablespoons flour, and sugar; stir to make a lump-free mixture. Allow this sponge to proof until bubbly and light. Combine remaining flour with salt and set aside.

Combine mashed potatoes with remaining 2 cups warm water (if you boiled the potatoes, use the potato water) until you have a lumpless soupy mixture the consistency of wallpaper paste. Make sure the potato mixture is about as hot as a baby's bottle (110°–115° F). If it is still too hot, allow it to cool until it feels comfortably warm. Add to yeast sponge.

With the mixer running, begin to work the flour in a cup at a time. Once you have a smooth mixture, turn dough out on a floured board and knead 15 minutes or until dough is supple. If dough seems sticky, add a little more flour. This dough must not be too soft or it will spread instead of rise. Make a stiff elastic dough. Oil mixing bowl, place dough ball in bowl, cover, and place in the warm, draft-free oven. Allow to rise until double in bulk (about 45 minutes).

Meanwhile, oil a 10-inch cast-iron skillet well. Once the dough has risen, remove from oven, punch down with your fist, turn out on the board, and knead for 2 minutes. Form a flattened round loaf and place it in the skillet. Coat top generously with oil or margarine, replace loaf in warm oven, and allow to rise again. This second rising will come up quickly, so don't overdo it. Begin checking after 25 minutes. When the loaf just begins coming up over the top, remove from the warm oven. Place loaf on top of the stove and preheat the oven to 400° F (takes about 10 minutes). If you have timed it just right, the loaf will now have risen about 1½ inches over the top of the skillet. Pop it into the hot oven and cook for 45 minutes to 1 hour, or until loaf is evenly brown and sounds hollow when tapped on the bottom. Cool on a rack. Do not attempt to cut this loaf until completely cooled (several hours). Best if you wait until the next day.

Twenty-Second Biscuits

▼

MAKES 12 BISCUITS IN 20 MINUTES
About 90¢ a panful

How many times have you heard those stories about biscuits that would melt in your mouth? How many times have you followed the recipe in some standard cookbook, only to wind up with dry clay dough? Here is a technique that circumvents the need for years of experience. It makes a flaky biscuit using a food processor.

1 small (5.33-ounce) can evaporated milk
1 tablespoon vinegar
water
2 cups flour
½ teaspoon salt
1 tablespoon sugar
¼ teaspoon soda
1 tablespoon baking powder
5 tablespoons shortening

Preheat oven to 450° F. Combine milk, vinegar, and enough water to make 1 cup of soured milk.

In the bowl of a food processor fitted with the plastic blade, combine dry ingredients. Process for about 5 seconds. Remove top of the container and evenly space the 5 tablespoons of shortening on top of the flour mixture. Replace top and process for 10 seconds. With the motor running, add sour milk. Process only until the mixture forms a rough ball (about 5 seconds).

Flour a dough board. Using a rubber spatula, remove dough ball to board. Flour your hands and pat the dough into a soft rectangle about 5x10 inches and about ½ inch thick. Cut with biscuit cutter to make about a dozen medium-sized biscuits.

Grease a 10x6-inch baking dish, then arrange biscuits with sides touching, and bake 12–15 minutes or until the tops are glistening golden. Take them to the table smoking hot.

Daddy's Corn Bread

▼

FEEDS 6 IN 35 MINUTES
About 40¢ per serving

This is no sissy, cake-sweet corn bread that comes out of a box. This is the real McCoy: coarse, pungent, satisfying. For a supper with greens, just add ¼–½ cup cooked ham or bacon to the batter before baking. Pass the syrup, please. For a Mexican variation, add corn and bell peppers. Dessert? Peaches and cream, naturally.

2 tablespoons vegetable oil
1 cup buttermilk
1 teaspoon salt
1 teaspoon baking soda
2 cups cornmeal
1 large egg

Put bacon grease into a 10-inch cast-iron skillet, place in oven set at 400° F, and heat to smoking.

Once oven is hot and grease is smoking, quickly stir together buttermilk, salt, and soda until a foam forms on surface. Stir in cornmeal and egg until smooth. Add sizzling bacon grease and stir. Pour mixture into hot skillet and bake uncovered for 30 minutes or until edges brown and center springs back to the touch.

Evelyne's Paper-thin Corn Bread

▼

FEEDS 6 IN 40 MINUTES
About 50¢ total

Since most of us work long hours, we don't want to think much about making bread. There are quick bread alternatives that are so easy to prepare, so cheap, and so delicious that you may get addicted to making them, even if you work out of the home all day and still consider baking a special treat.

The cost of this sheet of flat bread when made with real butter is about 50¢. This means that for less than a dime a serving you can have hot, fresh bread for supper, and you won't have to make a special trip to the grocery store for a long list of ingredients to make it. Your family will praise you. Trust me on this.

¾ cup yellow cornmeal
1 cup boiling water
½ teaspoon salt
3 tablespoons butter, melted

Preheat the oven to 400° F. Stir cornmeal into boiling water until it is smooth. Add salt and melted butter. Stir again.

Spread very thinly onto an ungreased cookie sheet. Bake about 30 minutes until crisp and browning. Break into odd-shaped pieces and serve warm.

> **CORN BREAD APPETIZERS**
> This bread makes a terrific hors d'oeuvre served plain or topped with cracked black pepper and Parmesan cheese. It's also a great dipper for pureed beans or salsa.

Focaccia

▼

FEEDS 4 IN 1½ HOURS
MAKES 1 14-INCH FLAT BREAD
About 40¢ per serving

3 cups bread flour
2 teaspoons salt
2½ teaspoons 50%-faster active dry yeast
⅞ cup hot tap water (120° F)
2 tablespoons olive oil plus extra for coating the top

Preheat oven to 500° F. (30 minutes if using a pizza stone or unglazed cooking tiles placed on the shelf in the bottom third of the oven.)

Using a food processor fitted with the steel blade, combine dry ingredients. Pulse to mix. Then with the motor running, add hot water and olive oil through the feed tube.
(continued)

Process until the dough begins to leave the side of the bowl. Knead for 60 seconds, adding flour as necessary if the dough seems sticky.

Remove the blade and the dough from the processor. Knead the dough on a lightly floured surface a moment, then roll it into a ball, and punch a hole in the middle like a donut. Replace the dough in the processor bowl. Cover with plastic wrap.

Raise dough in a warm, draft-free place or micro-rise until doubled in bulk.

Remove the dough from the processor bowl, punch it down, knead by hand a few seconds on a lightly floured board, then cover with the processor bowl and let it rest 10 minutes.

Meanwhile, sprinkle cornmeal on a round 15-inch piece of cardboard or a pizza peel. Roll the dough out on a lightly floured surface into a 14-inch circle about ⅓ inch thick. Transfer the dough to the cardboard or pizza peel and let it rise in a warm, draft-free place about 15 minutes until puffy and about ⅔ inch thick. Dimple the top of the bread with your fingertips, then wipe with additional olive oil and shovel onto a cooking stone or cookie sheet. Bake 15–20 minutes until the bread is an even golden brown. Remove to a rack to cool. Cut in wedges and serve warm or at room temperature.

Zucchini Bread

▼

MAKES 2 LOAVES IN 1 HOUR 10 MINUTES
About $1.00 per loaf

Some of these natural breads bear a striking resemblance to adobe bricks, but this version of zucchini bread is remarkably light.

3 large eggs
¾ cup vegetable oil
1 cup sugar
2 cups zucchini, grated fine
1 teaspoon vanilla
3 cups flour
1 teaspoon salt
1 teaspoon baking soda
½ teaspoon baking powder
1 teaspoon cinnamon
¾ cup chopped nuts or seeds
¾ cup dried fruit (raisins, chopped dates, prunes, or even grapes)

Preheat oven to 350° F. Mix eggs, oil, sugar, zucchini, and vanilla. Stir dry ingredients together. Add to liquid mixture. Mix thoroughly. Stir in nuts and fruit. Pour into two greased 8x4-inch loaf pans and bake for 50–60 minutes or until a toothpick inserted in center comes out clean. After you have allowed loaves to cool in the pans for 10 minutes, turn out on a rack.

Quick Coffee Cake

▼

FEEDS 6 IN 30 MINUTES
About 60¢ per serving

So I asked myself, what would Old Mother Hubbard have done if she'd had a nine o'clock appointment? There I stood at 7 A.M. in a kitchen bare of cereal, bacon, and bread. There was one egg. There was flour, looking more inert than ever. And off in the nether reaches of the house, distinct stirrings told me that the thundering herd would soon descend. I looked up and asked for the millionth time, why me? I, too, have to be somewhere at nine. There was no answer, so I threw it into high and here's what we had.

Cake:
¾ cup sugar
¼ cup shortening or oil
1 large egg
½ cup milk
1½ cups flour
2 teaspoons baking powder
½ teaspoon salt

Streusel Topping:
2 tablespoons melted margarine
½ cup brown sugar
2 tablespoons flour
2 teaspoons cinnamon
½ cup nuts, fruits, or oatmeal
Or
Simple Sugar Topping:
½ cup brown or white sugar
1½ teaspoons cinnamon

Preheat oven to 400° F. In a food processor or mixer, combine sugar, shortening, and egg. Then add remaining cake ingredients. Mix for about 10 seconds or until smooth.

Grease and flour a baking pan, either 10x6x1¾ inches or 9x9x1¾ inches. Spread batter in pan. Sprinkle one of the toppings on the cake evenly and bake about 20 minutes.

Pear Orange Bread

▼

MAKES 1 LOAF IN 1½ HOURS
About $1.50

1 winter pear, cored but not peeled
1–2 tablespoons lemon juice
½ cup fresh orange juice + zest from half an
* orange*
1 cup sugar
2 eggs
½ cup olive oil
3 cups flour
1 tablespoon baking powder
½ teaspoon baking soda
1½ teaspoons salt
1 teaspoon ground cinnamon
½ teaspoon nutmeg

Preheat the oven to 350° F. Grease a 9-inch glass loaf pan.

Fit the food processor with the grating disk. Grate the pear. Measure out ½ cup grated pear and place it in a medium-sized mixing bowl. Squeeze a little lemon juice over remaining grated pear to prevent darkening; set aside. (continued)

Pour orange juice and sugar over the ½ cup grated pear. Add orange zest, eggs, and oil. Whip with a fork to mix thoroughly. Set aside.

Wipe out the work bowl of the food processor and dry it. Fit food processor with the steel blade and mix dry ingredients in bowl. Pour the pear-orange-egg mixture over the dry ingredients. Barely mix by pulsing 5 or 6 times. Wipe down the sides of the work bowl with a rubber spatula and finish mixing by hand. (Less is more here. Overmix and the bread will be coarse, like people you know who've been beaten by life. Ruinous to quick bread and human beings, that beating.)

Turn this stiff batter into the prepared loaf pan. Bake on the middle rack about 1 hour or until golden brown on top (don't worry if it cracks). Insert a toothpick or skewer into the top. It should come out clean. Cool the bread in the pan 5 minutes on a rack, then turn it out of the pan and continue to cool on the rack.

Serve warm or at room temperature. That little dab of grated pear you have left over? Eat it with a fork, or spread it over slices of the bread, or fold it into whipped cream and serve a dollop atop each slice with a sprinkle of cinnamon or nutmeg. Good huh?

WHICH APPLES DO YOU COOK?
The Rome Beauty apple is far and away the best baking apple. Pippin and Golden Delicious are good, not only for baking, but for sauces and purees and top-of-the-stove preparations. If you need to choose an apple that won't turn brown too quickly—for those times when you are doing three things at once—stick with Golden Delicious. Jonathan and McIntosh apples cook well but tend to collapse in the oven, so these varieties are not suitable for any recipe which calls for the apple to maintain its shape. The one apple that is better for eating than cooking is Red Delicious.

Glazed Apple Slices
▼
FEEDS 4 IN 15 MINUTES
About 25¢ per serving

As good for breakfast as they are for dessert.

½ cup orange juice
⅓ cup light brown sugar
¼ teaspoon ground allspice
4 apples, unpeeled, cored and cut into rings

In a 10-inch skillet, combine orange juice, brown sugar, and allspice. Bring to a boil, stirring to dissolve sugar completely. Add apple rings, then simmer uncovered over low heat until tender, about 8–10 minutes. Spoon syrup over the apples during cooking and turn from time to time.

Apple Crisp

▼

FEEDS 8 IN 50 MINUTES
About 35¢ per serving

Even cold for breakfast, this is a good fruit-and-cereal combination that provides something more than empty calories and is full of fiber. This is a good recipe to experiment with. Raisins, nuts, and granola are interesting additions.

6 medium apples, unpeeled, cored and sliced thin
¾ cup plus 2 tablespoons brown sugar
1 teaspoon cinnamon
½ cup cornmeal
¾ cup rolled oats
¼ cup soft margarine

Preheat oven to 325° F. Using a little of the margarine, thoroughly grease a 10-inch cast-iron skillet. Arrange apple slices in skillet, then sprinkle with 2 tablespoons of the brown sugar and half the cinnamon.

Combine remaining brown sugar, cinnamon, cornmeal, and oats. Stir to mix completely. Cut in margarine and mash until you have a crumbly mixture. Sprinkle evenly over apples. Bake 30–35 minutes until topping is brown. Don't overcook. Serve warm. Good served warm with cream.

Almost Instant Apple Pie

▼

FEEDS 6–8 IN 35 MINUTES
About 40¢ per serving

Here is a good, quick, cheap version of an apple pie that goes together in 5 minutes flat.

½ cup sugar
2 tablespoons flour
¼ teaspoon nutmeg
¼ teaspoon cinnamon
4 baking apples (about 2 pounds), unpeeled, cored, and coarsely chopped
Juice of 1 lemon

Brown Sugar Crust:
1 cup flour
1 cup brown sugar
¼ pound butter or margarine

Preheat oven to 425° F. In a large deep bowl, combine sugar, flour, and spices. Toss apples with this mixture. Squeeze lemon juice over apples. Place coated apples in a 3-quart round baking dish.

For crust, combine flour and sugar. Cut in margarine. Sprinkle mixture over apples. Bake for 30 minutes. Serve warm in bowls with a little milk.

Plum Perfect Dessert

▼

FEEDS 6 IN 4 HOURS
(INCLUDES FREEZING TIME)
About 40¢ per serving

The French call these sorbets. The Italians call them granitas. I call them a bargain. A fruit ice is a trouble-free, delicious end to a summer meal. This combination works well when fruits are at the peak of the harvest, cheap and perfect.

1½ pounds ripe plums
1 pint fresh strawberries
1½ cups sugar
½ cup water
1 tablespoon lemon juice

Halve plums and remove pits. Hull strawberries. Combine fruits with sugar and water in saucepan. Bring to a boil, cover, and simmer about 5 minutes until plums are tender. Remove to processor or blender. Add lemon juice and puree until smooth. Pour into a 9-inch square pan, cover, and freeze until firm (about 4 hours).

If you find it too rocklike when you're ready to serve, either set it out of the freezer for 15 minutes or whirl it in the processor or blender for 10 seconds or so.

Fruit Granita

▼

FEEDS 4 IN 10 MINUTES
About 25¢ per serving

In Rome on street corners, vendors sell pureed fresh fruit and milk drinks made on the spot, tossing together grade C fruit, milk, and shaved ice. Refreshing and delicious. My neighbor and I tootled around the food processor until we came up with a taste that approximated her memory of the Roman drink. We froze what we couldn't drink on the spot, and that we called The Bush Street Granita. Either way, icy or frozen, you get a grainy fresh-fruit flavor. And, if you're lucky, once you're done you will have used up the bits and pieces of fresh fruit languishing in the back of your refrigerator.

2 cups mixed fresh fruit chunks (pears, apples, bananas, peaches, cantaloupe), cored and peeled
½ teaspoon cinnamon
½ teaspoon honey (or to taste)
1 cup ice cubes
2 cups milk
Cocoa for garnish

In a blender or food processor fitted with steel blade, combine fruit, cinnamon, and honey. Puree, tasting to adjust sweetness with more honey if you wish. With the motor running, drop the ice cubes through the feed tube and continue processing just until ice is completely chopped and incorporated. Pour milk through the feed tube and blend. Serve immediately in tall footed glasses, dusted with a little cocoa.

Winter Pear Pandowdy

▼

FEEDS 4 IN 45 MINUTES
About 50¢ each

Pandowdies originated in New England for using windfall fruits. Originally served for breakfast, it's still a great idea for a Sunday brunch. The name comes from the last recipe step when the crust, after a short baking time, is broken into pieces, pushed into the fruit, then returned to the oven to finish. Pushing the fruit down is called "dowdying."

4 cups pears, unpeeled, cored and sliced
Juice and zest of ½ lemon
1 cup pear nectar or apple juice
½ teaspoon ground cinnamon
½ teaspoon freshly grated nutmeg
1 cup flour
¼ teaspoon salt
½ cup butter or margarine
3 tablespoons ice water
2 teaspoons milk
1 tablespoon sugar
Frozen yogurt or ice cream on the side

Grease an 8-inch pan. Preheat the oven to 350° F. Toss pears with lemon juice and zest. Place in the pan, pour the nectar over, and set aside.

In the food processor bowl fitted with steel blade, combine the cinnamon, nutmeg, flour, and salt. Pulse to mix. Open the lid and cut the butter over the top. Process about 10 seconds, until the mixture resembles coarse meal. With the motor running, pour the ice water and milk through the feed tube. Process just until the mixture is crumbly. Sprinkle over the pears. Sprinkle with sugar.

Bake about 30 minutes, until bubbly and brown. Using a spoon, knock the crust down into the fruit for the last 10 minutes of cooking. To serve, cut into 4-inch squares and serve each with a dollop of frozen yogurt or ice cream.

Micro-Poached Peaches

▼

FEEDS 4 IN 30 MINUTES
About 50¢ each

4 ripe fresh peaches
Juice of ½ lemon
2 tablespoons sugar
1 cup water
1-inch piece of cinnamon stick
(continued)

1 whole clove
½ cup whipping cream
¼ cup powdered sugar
½ teaspoon vanilla
Mint leaves for garnish

Peel peaches if you wish. Cut a small bit away from the bottom of the peach so that it will stand without falling over, then slip each one into a bowl of water in which you have squeezed the lemon juice. Reserve.

Combine in a 1-quart glass measure the sugar, water, cinnamon stick, and clove. Microwave uncovered at 100% (HIGH) for 1½ minutes. Cover the syrup with plastic wrap and microwave at 100% (HIGH) 3 minutes more. Carefully remove the plastic wrap.

Arrange the peaches in a microwaveable 9-inch pie plate or souffle dish, pour the syrup over the peaches, cover with plastic wrap, and microwave at 100% (HIGH) for 4 minutes. Carefully lift the plastic wrap and spoon the syrup over the peaches. Recover and microwave at 100% (HIGH) for 4 more minutes.

Cool to room temperature. Cover and refrigerate 2 hours or until serving time. Discard cinnamon and clove. Whip cream to soft peaks, season with powdered sugar and vanilla. Serve each peach in a pool of syrup, top with whipped cream and finish with a sprig of mint.

Easy Fruit Cobbler
▼
FEEDS 8 IN 1 HOUR
About 50¢ per serving

The best thing about a cobbler is that it's so easy to put together. You can have it in the oven before the fresh-picked berries have lost their warmth from the sun. It's easier than pie with no crust to roll out, and with fresh-picked fruit, the whole thing becomes ridiculously cheap besides being so good.

This method can be used with most any fruit, depending on the season. Peaches, nectarines, cherries—sweet or sour, all kinds of berries. In the winter, use pears or apples, and toss in some nuts if you've got 'em. The idea here is a biscuitlike pastry dappled with butter-laden fruit. Pass the cream, please.

1½ cups fresh blackberries or other fruit of the
    season, cut into bite-sized chunks
1 cup sugar
½ cup unsalted butter or margarine
1 cup flour
1 teaspoon baking powder
½ teaspoon salt
½ cup milk

Preheat the oven to 400° F. Wash and prepare fruit. Place fruit in a bowl and toss with ½ cup (or to taste) sugar. (Canned fruit will not require this additional sugar.) Set aside.

Melt butter in a 9x13-inch baking dish in the oven.
(continued)

Combine dry ingredients in a medium-ized bowl. Add milk and mix just until mooth.

Remove baking dish from the oven, and pread the melted butter to completely cover he bottom and up the sides. Weave the batter nto the pan, leaving spaces where only butter hows. Fill those spaces with fruit. Pile the ruit up high into those spots, sugar syrup and ll. Bake about 35 minutes until the cobbler is rown around the edges and the sugar is eginning to caramelize in the spaces. Serve varm in bowls, and pass a pitcher of cold, eavy cream or milk.

Faux Cherry Pie

▼

FEEDS 8 IN 1 HOUR
About 40¢ each

This recipe comes from the depression days vhen people freely made substitutions. Since his pie tastes so good, you may want to emember to stock up on 12-ounce bags of ranberries and throw them in the freezer. They'll keep for most of the year, and you'll probably find other good uses for them besides pie. Call this pie what you will. By any other name, it smells the same: divine.

Crust:
½ cup roasted peanuts, finely ground
1½ cups old-fashioned rolled oats
¼ cup flour
¾ cup brown sugar, firmly packed
2 teaspoons cinnamon
½ teaspoon nutmeg
¼ teaspoon salt
½ cup soft butter or margarine

Filling:
2 cups whole raw cranberries
¾ cup sugar
1 tablespoon flour
1 teaspoon almond extract
1½ teaspoons butter or margarine

Vanilla ice cream (optional)

Preheat the oven to 475° F. For crust, blend thoroughly in a medium bowl all crust ingredients except butter. Then cut in butter until the mixture resembles coarse meal. Press half the mixture into a 9-inch pie plate.

For filling, place cranberries over crust. Combine sugar and flour and sprinkle over the berries. Sprinkle almond flavoring on top, then dot with butter.

Pour remaining crust over top of berries, smoothing as much as you can. Bake for 10 minutes, then reduce the heat to 425° F and bake about 30 minutes more until the crust is bubbly and brown. Cool thoroughly, then scoop out servings onto dessert dishes and top with vanilla ice cream.

Holiday Fancies

▼

MAKES 75 IN 30 MINUTES
About $1.50 a batch

It's the Fourth of July, and you're invited to the block party. Bring something, they say. How about a cookie reduced to its barest essentials? Here's a delicious shortcake that's accented by whatever topping you can find. If you can afford to try these with real butter, you'll find them so good you'll fall to your knees.

1 cup sugar
2 sticks butter or margarine
1 egg
3½ cups flour
Topping (jam, nuts, nonpareils, cinnamon,
    sugar)

Preheat oven to 300° F. Grease two cookie sheets well. Cut butter into sugar until mixture resembles coarse meal. Add egg and blend completely. Now add flour and mix to make a very short, crumbly dough. (All can be done in processor in 2 minutes.) Using a tablespoon for a mold, press dough firmly into the bowl so that you have an egg-shaped piece in the spoon. Now slide the cookie onto the cookie sheet. Repeat until you have used all the dough. Make an indentation in each cookie with your index finger. Using the little spoon, drop a dab of topping into each hole (jam, an almond, a walnut or pecan half, cinnamon and sugar).

Bake about 15 minutes until edges are brown. Let stand on cookie sheet 2–3 minutes then remove to a rack for cooling. Store in tin, separating layers with waxed paper.

Bare Bones Sugar Cookies

▼

MAKES 2 DOZEN IN 15 MINUTES
About 75¢ a batch

⅓ cup shortening
½ cup sugar
¼ teaspoon vanilla or other flavoring
1 egg
¾ cup flour
½ teaspoon baking powder
Pinch of salt
½ cup nuts, seeds, raisins, or chocolate
    chips (optional)

Preheat oven to 350° F. Mix the shortening and sugar until light and fluffy. Add vanilla and egg and mix thoroughly. Now add flour, baking powder, and salt. Stir to mix with a fork. Add nuts if desired.

Drop by teaspoonfuls onto a greased cookie sheet. Sprinkle tops with sugar. Bake about 15 minutes until edges brown. Cool on a rack.

Meringues

▼

MAKES ABOUT 24 LARGE
IN 1 HOUR 15 MINUTES
About 10¢ a cookie

3 egg whites
½ teaspoon cream of tartar
½ cup sugar
¼ teaspoon vanilla or other flavoring
½ cup nuts, chocolate chips, marshmallows, or
   fruit bits, or ¼ cup unsweetened cocoa

Preheat oven to 250° F. Beat egg whites with cream of tartar until foamy, then begin adding sugar, a teaspoon at a time, until you have stiff peaks. Add vanilla or fold in nuts, raisins, or even chocolate chips.

Now put a grocery sack on a cookie sheet and drop the stiff meringue onto the paper by the heaping teaspoonful. If you want a "nest" for fruit or ice cream, make an indentation with the back of the spoon. Bake for 1 hour. Gently peel off the paper while warm. Cool on a rack. Store in a tin (these keep well).

Microwave Flan Almendra

▼

FEEDS 4 IN 30 MINUTES
About 45¢ each

Making custards in the microwave is simple, provided you remember to turn the power back to 50%. Use a too-hot setting, and the custard will curdle. You can flavor this basic egg custard with other things besides almonds, if you wish. Lemon or orange zest. A whiff of espresso. Any way you make it, this is an easy custard to serve for Christmas or family-night dinners.

1¼ cup milk
4 large eggs
⅓ cup sugar
1 teaspoon vanilla extract
1 teaspoon almond extract (optional)
4 tablespoons slivered almonds

Microwave the milk in a 1-quart microwaveable bowl at 100% (HIGH) for 2 minutes.

Meanwhile, in another bowl, whisk together the eggs, sugar, and vanilla and almond extracts. Pour in the hot milk and stir to mix.

Place a tablespoon of slivered almonds in each of 4½-cup ramekins. Pour custard into ramekins. Arrange the ramekins evenly on a microwave carousel. Microwave at 50% (MEDIUM) for 6–7 minutes until firm.

Remove and cool. Serve at room temperature or chilled.

> **OPTIONAL FLAVORS**
> If you don't like the taste of almond, substitute other flavors: the zest of ½ orange, ½ teaspoon of instant powdered espresso, or for an old-fashioned American baked custard taste, sprinkle with cinnamon and grate a little nutmeg over each before baking.

Granny's Favorite Cake

▼

FEEDS 8 IN 1½ HOURS
About 75¢ each

½ cup unsalted butter or margarine, softened
2 cups sugar
2 large eggs, beaten to a froth
2 cups sifted cake flour
2 teaspoons soda
2 teaspoons cinnamon
1 teaspoon ginger
½ teaspoon salt
4 cups winter pears or apples, peeled, cored,
    and sliced
1 cup golden raisins
1 cup pecan, chopped
Whipped cream, sweetened with powdered
    sugar and vanilla, for garnish

Preheat the oven to 350° F. Grease and flour a 9x13-inch baking dish; set aside.

In processor bowl fitted with the steel blade, cream together butter, sugar, eggs. Open the lid and add dry ingredients. Pulse 5–6 times to mix. Fold in pears, raisins, and nuts using a rubber spatula. Turn into prepared pan.

Bake about 50 minutes, until cake is well-risen, golden brown and firm to the touch. Remove from the oven, cool in the pan on a wire rack. Serve plain or with a dollop of sweetened whipped cream.

CHEAP CHOCOLATE THAT TASTES GREAT

Sometimes nothing but chocolate will do. If you've priced baking chocolate squares or chips lately, you know that a 12-ounce container can push upwards of $2. Since most chocolate-based cakes and brownies require at least 2 squares, that means the chocolate alone in a recipe could cost you 35¢ or better.

The bargain in the chocolate business is good old-fashioned cocoa. Last week, I picked up an 8-ounce container of the house brand for 87¢. For brownies, that brings the chocolate cost down to a measly dime for a good main-line hit of chocolate in a mouthwatering dessert. And cocoa allows you to control the fat in a recipe since you add fat to mimic prepared chocolate bars or chips. If your favorite chocolate dessert calls for baking chocolate you can always substitute either using a standard conversion or whacking away at the fat content by shaving off the amount of shortening you add to the cocoa.

Plain chocolate syrup is a staple in the homes where most children reside. Why don't you and your kids make it together? You'll save money. You'll begin teaching your kids to cook. You'll have on hand the beginnings for chocolate milk, ice cream topping, even a swirl to top fresh fruit.

Transform that syrup into hot-fudge sauce with the easy recipe that follows, and you've stepped into the category of sublime. And all for about 25% of what it costs to buy the stuff already prepared, and made in the microwave it doesn't even take too much time. (See recipes on the next page.)

Homemade Chocolate Syrup

▼

MAKES 2 CUPS IN 3 MINUTES
About $1.15

7 tablespoons cocoa
1 cup sugar
¾ cup evaporated milk
¼ cup butter
⅛ teaspoon salt
½ teaspoon vanilla

Combine in a 1-quart microwaveable dish the cocoa, sugar, and milk; whisk together. Cook in the microwave at 100% (HIGH) for 1 minute. Remove and stir in the butter and salt. Replace in the microwave and cook at 100% (HIGH) power for 1 minute 30 seconds more. Remove and stir in the vanilla. Whisk thoroughly. Pour into a sterile jar, cover, and refrigerate.

Hot-Fudge Sauce

▼

MAKES 2 CUPS IN 4 MINUTES
About $1.35

This is that sauce that cracks when you spoon it over ice cream making a shell so delicious, it will transport you to wherever it is that good chocolate takes you when you want to be taken.

½ cup homemade chocolate syrup
½ cup butter
1 cup powdered sugar

Combine chocolate syrup and butter in a 1-quart microwaveable dish. Heat in the microwave at 100% (HIGH) for 1 minute.

Remove and beat with a wire whisk to combine. Then whisk in the powdered sugar and replace in the microwave. Heat for 2 minutes at 100% (HIGH), whisk again, then pour into a sterile glass jar. Store, covered in the refrigerator. To reheat, remove the metal lid and place in the microwave on 100% (HIGH) for about 30 seconds, until bubbly.

TRY A SUNDAE PIE
Make an instant sundae pie by beginning with a graham cracker crust, fill it with best quality vanilla ice cream, drizzle fudge sauce over that, then heap the top with fresh sliced strawberries.

Busy-Day Brownies

▼

MAKES 9 SQUARES IN 30 MINUTES
About 35¢ each

Here are brownies dense as fudge, deeper chocolate than a Hershey bar, and easy as pie. Since they don't call for expensive butter or chocolate, they're cheap to make. If you have nuts and chocolate chips you can gild this lily, but you'll find them delicious—as is. They're also a 1-bowl mixture for easy clean up. Pour yourself a tall glass of icy-cold milk to wash it all down.

½ cup nut pieces (optional)
2 large eggs
1 cup sugar
1 teaspoon vanilla
½ cup vegetable oil
¼ teaspoon salt
¼ teaspoon baking powder
⅓ cup cocoa
½ cup flour, unsifted
½ cup semisweet chocolate chips (optional)

Preheat the oven to 375° F. Grease a 9-inch square baking pan. Sprinkle the pan with nuts if desired; set aside.

Combine the ingredients in order in a large bowl, beating after each addition. Finally, sprinkle the flour evenly over the top of the mixture. Stir just until the flour is barely mixed in.

Pour the mixture into the pan, smoothing the batter evenly over the nuts. Bake 25–30 minutes until the center is cooked or a toothpick inserted in the middle comes out barely moist.

Remove the brownies from the oven and sprinkle with chocolate chips. Once melted, smooth them evenly over the top for the simplest icing you ever made. Cut into squares and serve warm.

Stocking the $10-a-Day Kitchen

▼

Cooks today are virtually assailed with new equipment. However, you needn't run out and buy anything to become a better cook. You just need to cook and taste and practice, using whatever pots and pans you have. If you got those pots and pans at a garage sale, good for you. You'd be amazed what people discard chasing this dream of perfection through products.

I am the weakest willed of all. Over time, I have bought for myself a microwave, a food processor, a crock pot, a coffee grinder and a bread machine. I'm too embarrassed to give you the whole profligate list. I use every one of these tools. I move them back and forth on the cabinet, wiping up crumbs and coffee grounds that nest beneath them. I like them. They're as much fun as an electric train or a chemistry set. They do save time. But they haven't made me a better cook. Cooking has made me a better cook.

If you have a 2-burner hotplate, a skillet, and a 3-quart saucepan, you're in business. Add some wooden spoons, measuring cups and spoons, and you're halfway home. With a big bowl to beat and mix things in, you don't have to wash out the saucepan to whip the cream. The equipment you can buy is endless (thanks to the fertile imaginations of marketing men). Indulge yourself when you feel like it. Play with the new toys you bring home. Fancy equipment does make cooking fun, but care and attention make fine cuisine.

The proof is in the pudding, as they say, and whatever inventiveness you have been forced to resort to in order to achieve that fabled pudding will simply add to the satisfaction you feel when you see that faraway look come over the face of the person you have cooked for. The look that tells you all of the diner's attention is focused on the pleasure from that first fantastic bite. Whatever carnage lies behind the achievement of that magical moment is of no concern to cook or diner as they sit together to enjoy the food.

Nobody cares whether a good book was composed on a word processor or an ancient Underwood. So it is with cooking. Create the masterpiece and your audience will never even think about the cost of ingredients or the sophistication of the equipment. Their attention will be on pleasure. And that's what good cooking can provide.

Since the art of substitution is basic to budget cuisine, this chapter lists some common substitutions that can be made. In some cases, you might substitute a more costly ingredient for a cheaper one if that's what you have on hand. The idea is to keep you inventing from the contents of your own pantry. This is not to say that the results will be identical. That isn't even a reasonable goal. But remember that you may create a dish that is better than the original was.

For the cook, substituting can be even more exciting than following the recipe to the letter. It gives you the sense that you invented something, and that keeps you interested.

Here are the items to have on hand to keep you from impulsive trips to the store.

Fresh Herbs and Seasonings:
Apples
Bell pepper
Carrots
Celery
Garlic cloves
Ginger root
Lemons
Lettuce
Onions
Parsley

Canned Goods:
Beef broth
Chicken broth
Clams
Evaporated milk
Tomato products (stewed tomatoes, sauce, and paste)
Tuna fish

Dried Goods:
Baking powder
Baking soda
Cornmeal
Cornstarch
Flour
Powdered milk
Raisins or prunes
Sugar (white granulated, powdered, and brown)
Salt

Condiments:
Catsup
Honey
Mayonnaise

Mustard
Oils (cottonseed, olive, sesame, peanut)
Pickles
Salad dressing
Soy sauce
Tabasco sauce
Vanilla
Vinegar
Worcestershire sauce

Herbs and Seasonings:
Allspice
Basil
Bay leaves
Bouillon cubes
Chili powder
Cinnamon
Cloves
Cumin
Curry powder
Dill
Garlic powder
Ginger
Nutmeg
Oregano
Paprika
Pepper (red and black)
Peppercorns
Poppy seeds
Poultry seasoning
Rosemary
Sage
Savory
Sesame seeds
Tarragon
Thyme
(continued)

Staples:
Bread
Crackers
Dried beans
Rice (white and brown)
Oatmeal or cream of wheat
Pastas (macaroni, spaghetti, rotini, ramen)
Shortening
Tortillas (corn and flour)

From the Refrigerator:
Cheese (cheddar, cream, Parmesan)
Eggs
Butter and margarine
Milk
Yogurt or sour cream

Storing Food

When fruits and vegetables are at peak harvest, bulk prices are often too tempting to refuse. If you have the means to store, this is the time to buy. Potatoes and onions store best laid out one layer deep in a cool, dark place—not in the refrigerator. A basement room, cellar, a dark corner of the garage are all good places.

You can freeze as much corn on the cob as your freezer will hold by simply placing the unshucked ears in double layers of those black plastic garbage liners and heaving the whole thing into the freezer. The corn won't be as sweet as it was the day you brought it home, but the husk acts as a natural barrier against freezer burn. You can also double-wrap whole bell peppers and freeze them. They will not be suitable for eating raw, but work admirably in sauces through the winter.

I once tried to freeze a big sack of onions. It was a disaster. Some people tell me they chop and freeze onions. I can't see any sense in this, since onions are inherently stable and will keep, whole, for months in a cool, dark place. They tell me you can keep carrots all winter if you stick them in sand in a dark place. However, somebody would have to give me the carrots before I'd go to the trouble and expense of hauling sand to a dark spot.

If you buy fresh ginger root, store it the way the Chinese do. Simply stick the whole root in a clay pot filled with sandy, rich earth, then water it as you would water a cactus. It keeps indefinitely. Whole garlic pods needn't be refrigerated. Store them in an opaque, aerated, covered jar at room temperature.

Olive oil keeps best in an opaque container in a cool, dark place, but not in the refrigerator. I buy gallon cans and keep it in the pantry, which is moderately cool. I have never had any go rancid using this method. Refrigerated olive oil becomes cloudy.

If you use only part of a can of any food product, especially tomatoes, transfer the remainder to a glass or plastic container before refrigerating. Tomato eats the can in three days. To store lettuce, wet a paper towel and wrap the base of the lettuce in the damp paper towel, then replace it in the plastic bag and place in the hydrator section. Lettuce keeps a month stored in this manner. To ripen an avocado in a hurry, place it inside a canister filled with flour. Leave it 24 hours and, voila, a ripe avocado.

Substitutions

CONDIMENTS

Barbecue Sauce (1 cup) =
1 cup catsup
Dash of Tabasco sauce
1 tablespoon Worcestershire
1 tablespoon mustard
1½ tablespoons oil
Salt and pepper
Mix and simmer 10 minutes.

Catsup (½ cup) =
½ cup tomato sauce
2 tablespoons brown sugar
1 tablespoon vinegar
⅛ teaspoon ground cloves

Chili Sauce (½ cup) =
same as above plus:
1 garlic clove, pressed
1 tablespoon chili powder
Simmer 5 minutes.

Mustard (1 teaspoon dry) =
1 tablespoon prepared

Seafood Cocktail Sauce (1 cup) =
½ cup catsup
½ cup chili sauce
1 tablespoon horseradish
Juice of half a lemon

Soy Sauce (¼ cup) =
3 tablespoons Worcestershire sauce
1 tablespoon water

Tabasco Sauce =
Cayenne (red) pepper

Teriyaki Sauce (1 tablespoon) =
1 teaspoon soy sauce
1 teaspoon white wine
1 teaspoon sesame oil
½ clove garlic, pressed
¼ teaspoon ginger, fresh-grated

Worcestershire Sauce (1 teaspoon) =
1 tablespoon soy sauce
¼ teaspoon sugar
Dash of Tabasco

FLAVORINGS

Bread Crumbs
¼ cup dry crumbs = 1 slice bread or
½ cup soft crumbs = 1 slice bread or
1 cup dry crumbs = ¾ cup cracker crumbs

(continued)

Chocolate
Unsweetened (1 ounce square) =
3 tablespoons cocoa
1 tablespoon shortening

Semisweet (1⅔ ounces) =
1 ounce square unsweetened
4 teaspoons sugar

Semisweet Chocolate Chips or Squares
(6 ounces) =
6 tablespoons cocoa,
7 tablespoons sugar
¼ cup shortening

Unsweetened Liquid Baking Chocolate
(1 ounce) =
3 tablespoons cocoa
1 tablespoon vegetable oil

Coffee (½ cup) =
1 teaspoon instant coffee
½ cup water

Lemon Juice (1 teaspoon) =
¼ teaspoon vinegar

Nuts
Walnuts, Pecans, Peanuts, Almonds =
Sesame seeds, pumpkin seeds, poppyseeds

Raisins =
Prunes (Plump prunes in boiling water.)
Dates
(Seed prunes and dates.)

Wine (½ cup dry) =
¼ cup vinegar
1 tablespoon sugar
¼ cup water

Vermouth, dry sherry, or dry white wine can be used interchangeably in most recipes. A hearty burgundy is a good choice for brown sauces, but ruins spaghetti sauce. Do not buy cooking wine, which is salty and costs too much by the ounce. Stick to cheap, reliable jug wines.

HERBS

1 tablespoon fresh leaves=
   1 teaspoon crushed, dried herbs OR
   ⅔ teaspoon powdered herbs

Allspice (1 teaspoon ground) =
½ teaspoon ground cinnamon
⅛ teaspoon ground cloves

Bay Leaf (1 dried leaf) =
¼ teaspoon crushed leaves

Chili Powder =
New Mexico red chili powder, ground comino, finely milled black pepper, ground oregano, and garlic powder. Mix to taste in declining volume from first ingredient to last.

Garlic (1 clove fresh, pressed)=
   ⅛ teaspoon garlic powder OR
   1 teaspoon garlic salt OR
   ½ teaspoon garlic flakes

Ginger (1 tablespoon fresh-grated)=
  ⅛ teaspoon powdered ginger OR
  1 tablespoon candied ginger with sugar
  rinsed off

Onion (1 small fresh, minced)=
  1 tablespoon instant, minced OR
  ¼ cup frozen, chopped

Parsley (¼ cup fresh, cut fine) =
  1 tablespoon dried parsley

LEAVENING AGENTS

Baking Powder (1 teaspoon)=
  ¼ teaspoon baking soda+
  ⅝ teaspoon cream of tartar OR
  ¼ teaspoon baking soda+
  ½ cup yogurt or buttermilk OR
  ¼ teaspoon baking soda+
  ¼ cup molasses

Yeast (1 package dry)=
  1 cake compressed yeast OR
  1 tablespoon dry bulk yeast OR
  1 cup sourdough starter

SWEETENERS

Granulated sugar (1 cup)=
  ¾ cup honey (reduce liquid in recipe by ¼
  cup) OR
  2 cups corn syrup (never use more than half
  corn syrup as replacement for sugar in a
  recipe; reduce liquid for each cup of corn
  syrup by ¼ cup) OR

¾ cup maple syrup (reduce liquid by 3
  tablespoons) OR
1 cup brown sugar OR
1 cup superfine sugar OR
1¾ cups powdered sugar (do not substitute
  or baking) OR
1 cup Turbinado OR
1¼ cups molasses (decrease liquid in recipe
  by ¼ cup; substitute ½ teaspoon baking
  soda or baking powder in recipe)

THICKENERS

Flour (1 tablespoon)=
  1½ teaspoons cornstarch, potato starch,
  or arrowroot OR
  2 teaspoons tapioca OR
  1 beaten egg (combined with warm liquid,
  then added back to sauce)

MILK AND CREAM

Milk (1 cup whole homogenized)=
  ⅓ cup dry powdered milk+
  ¾ cup water (no fat) OR
  ½ cup evaporated milk+
  ½ cup water OR
  (in baking) 1 cup buttermilk+
  ½ teaspoon soda (decrease baking powder by
  2 teaspoons)

Sour milk (1 cup)=
  1 cup yogurt OR
  1 cup buttermilk OR
  1 tablespoon vinegar or lemon juice, enough
  sweet milk to equal 1 cup. Let stand 5
  minutes to clabber.
(continued)

159

Cream, Whipping (1 cup)=
⅓ cup butter+
¾ cup milk (will not whip, use for sauces only) OR
⅔ cup ice-cold evaporated milk (whips to equal volume as 1 cup whipping cream) OR
1 cup nonfat dry milk powder+
1 cup ice-water. Whip in a bowl nested in an ice-water bath.

Half-and-Half (1 cup)=
⅞ cup milk+
3 tablespoons butter OR
½ cup milk+
½ cup whipping cream OR
¾ cup evaporated milk+
¼ cup water

Sour Cream (1 cup)=
⅓ cup butter+
¾ cup buttermilk or yogurt OR
1 cup pureed cottage cheese+
¼ cup yogurt or buttermilk OR
6 ounces cream cheese and enough yogurt to yield 1 cup OR
An equal amount of yogurt or buttermilk can be used in a recipe calling for sour cream.
Note lower butterfat content in the final product. Lower cost and fewer calories.

VEGETABLES

Celery =
Mature chard stems

Mushrooms (1 pound fresh)=
3 ounces dried mushrooms OR
12 ounces canned mushrooms OR

3 cups raw = 1 cup cooked

Spinach =
Lettuce, romaine, iceberg, etc.

Tomatillos =
Green tomatoes

Tomatoes (1 cup canned)=
1⅓ cup chopped fresh tomatoes simmered 10 minutes OR
½ cup tomato sauce+
1 cup water

Tomato Juice (1 cup)
½ cup tomato sauce+
½ cup water OR
1 6-ounce can paste+
3 cans water+
salt+
sugar

Tomato Sauce (2 cups) =
¾ cup tomato paste
1 cup water

Tomato Soup (1 can) =
1 cup tomato sauce
½ cup milk or water

Tomato Paste (1 tablespoon) =
1 tablespoon catsup

Tomato Puree (1 cup) =
½ cup tomato paste
½ cup water

Water Chestnuts =
Jerusalem artichokes (sunchokes) peeled and steamed 5 minutes

What To Do with a Half a Can of Tomato Sauce and Other Conundrums

I've been taking a lot of heat lately for suggesting recipes that might call for a half a can of tomato sauce, or a partial container of tomato paste.

How dare I call it thrift if I've opened a can of something and had some left over? What is the frugal cook to do?

In the first place, whenever you look at any recipe, you have to inventory your own pantry to see if you have all the ingredients—or nearly all. Secondly, you have to decide if you agree with the cook who offers a recipe, and decide if you like the suggestions for ingredients.

If I had a recipe for soup offered me, for example, and it called for one and one half cans of tomato sauce, I'd do one of several things. I'd follow the recipe to the letter, and pour the other half of the tomato sauce down the drain. Good god. I only paid 25 cents for a can of the stuff, so what if I toss 12½¢ away? It's one choice. Sometimes better down the drain than down the gullet.

Second, I'd more than likely just pour the whole can of tomato sauce into the concoction on the theory that if a little's good a lot is better.

Third, I might decide not to open that second can of tomato sauce at all and to substitute a couple of tablespoons of tomato catsup, or a blob of tomato paste or, if my garden is flush, I'd just whack some fresh tomatoes into the soup.

Regardless of the decision I made, I'd taste the recipe as I went along to make sure it suited me. What any recipe provider is offering you is a guide to combining flavors, textures, scents, and temperature to come up with a pleasing creation. It's up to you to become an active participant in the process by tasting as you go along and really thinking about what you do like and what you don't.

The very last thing I'd do is attempt to save a half can of tomato sauce. How? Where? Why? If I put it in a little plastic container, label it, and freeze it, I can use it again provided I can: a.) remember that I have it, b.) remember how much it is, and c.) find it in a freezer cluttered with little blobs of other leftover ingredients that might better have gone into the dish, the dog, or the trash.

If I put the half can in the refrigerator, I can use it in a day or so, but not longer because the can will give the tomato sauce an off-taste. If I transfer it to a glass container, I can store it in the refrigerator somewhat longer wherein the same a-b-c possibilities mentioned in the last paragraph apply plus an additional d.) possibility: the tomato sauce will grow green hair and may even salute when I open the lid to the jar.

Whenever you are working with recipes that somebody suggested, keep in mind

Eckhardt's cardinal rule of substitution: never let the lack of ingredients keep you from trying a recipe. Substitute. Taste. Who knows? You might come up with a better recipe than the one that was handed you.

It's the whole thrill of cooking. You get to juggle ingredients, times, temperatures, techniques. You get to be an artist in your own kitchen, a scientist in your own home laboratory. What could be more fun?

The Top Ten Uses For a Half a Can of Tomato Sauce

10. Dump it in the recipe anyway.
9. Clean the drains by pouring it down the sink.
8. Take it by the spoonful for a spring tonic.
7. Make an instant pizza using this on an English muffin with the usual toppings.
6. Fertilize your houseplants.
5. Pour over pasta or eat it for lunch.
4. Rinse the greenish cast out of blond hair.
3. Make homemade V-8 juice.
2. Polish copper pots.
1. Make a great Bloody Mary.

Index

▼